The A Credible Business Communication

The Art of Credible Business Communication

Is This Book for You? – Checklist

I do not want you to purchase and read this book if it doesn't help you, or if you already know exactly how to appear entirely credible to every single person in every single situation.

So, let me tell you who this book is not for.

If you do not believe that you need to convey credibility to succeed in your career – no matter what industry you are in – then this book is not for you.

If you do not believe that you can exert a tremendous amount of control over your perceived credibility – by applying proven psychological and cognitive principles to your communication – then this book is not for you.

If you do not want to turn every meeting, interview, or presentation that will inevitably occur in your career into an opportunity for advancement, then this book is not for you.

And now, let me tell you who this book *is* for.

This book is for you if you want to excel in your professional career.

This book is for you if you want to discover a proven framework that can make your communication vastly more credible to your listeners.

This book is for you if you find yourself needing to convince others of the validity of your ideas in your line of work.

This book is for you if you have an upcoming interview, or if you are job hunting, and want to ace the interview with stunning ease and get your dream job by conveying credibility to the decision-maker.

This book is for you if you want to earn a promotion in your current workplace by creating the strong perception that you are to be trusted, simply because of the way you speak.

This book is for you if you want to exert more influence with more ease over the people you encounter in your career by getting total trust and cultivating complete credibility.

This book is for you if you want to learn these critical concepts free from unimportant anecdotes, irrelevant side-notes, and an unnecessary amount of words.

This book is for you if you are ambitious; if you want to maximize your potential, achieve your goals, and have a fruitful and rewarding career.

Don't believe me? Let me explain why credibility is so important.

Why Credibility?

Let me tell you exactly why credibility is so important to you.

Virtually every single person who has achieved worldly success – a fruitful career, a thriving business, or a respectable reputation – agrees with one thing.

And what's that?

That credibility is crucial.

Think about what success demands from you.

Success demands that you can convey your ideas to a neutral party and convince them that they should do something in your (and their) favor.

Success demands that your employee can trust you with opportunities that come across his or her desk.

Success demands that you can change minds and influence people without excessive hype, coercion, or manipulation.

Success demands that you can build a reputation that instantly makes anyone want to work *with* you rather than *against* you.

Success demands that you can make yourself believed when you are informing anyone of anything.

Success demands that you are not only an expert, but someone who can *talk* like an expert, and get the trust and authority you deserve.

Success demands that you are confident in your communication.

Success demands that your business writing, your presentations, or any piece of communication you produce in your career carries with it the infallible perception that it is to be trusted and treated with respect, not tossed aside.

If you don't see where I'm going with this, I'll tell you right now.

Every single thing required for a successful career and life is possible with credibility, and significantly harder, if not impossible, without it.

And my humble promise to you is this: by the end of this short book, you will unlock over 450 scientifically proven, simple, step-by-step strategies that are not manipulative or coercive, for achieving the fundamental prerequisite to success: massive credibility.

It is a different world when you prove your ideas with ease.

It is a different world when your listeners, whether they are colleagues, prospects, customers, prospective employers, or promotional committees, leave their conversation with you thinking, "wow... this person knows what's going on. I'm impressed."

It is a different world when you understand how to appeal to human psychology and cognitive functions to get what you want without manipulating people into working against their best interests.

It is a different world when a once exhausting endeavor becomes easy simply because people trust you, what you say, what you stand for, and what you propose.

It is a different world when communicating your ideas is not nerve-wracking, but a source of confidence.

It is a different world when changing minds and influencing people – once an obstacle – is now a stepping stone to success.

It is a different world when you master, fully and fluently, the single skill that is, above all else, the prerequisite to a successful career and life.

But why else is credibility so important for a successful career?

Think about it: the same words spoken by two different people can carry dramatically different impacts on those who hear them.

Right? Haven't you noticed?

If you've spent any time in boardrooms, you'll notice something: someone says something, and it gets brushed aside, barely acknowledged, thrown into the dustbin. Someone proposes an idea, and it is dead on arrival. *That someone is probably struggling twice as hard to accomplish the same goals. That someone is probably experiencing tremendous frustration at the stagnation of their career.*

And then something incredible happens.

What's that?

Someone else speaks up and conveys a roughly identical idea as that first person.

What ensues?

"Brilliant!"

"I think that's what we've been missing this entire time..."

"You're right. Let's do that."

"Exactly! I couldn't have said it better myself."

"Your expert judgment comes in handy once again. Great work. Meeting adjourned."

Now, why am I telling you this?

I am telling you this because this all-too-common scenario plays out constantly, every single day, in the offices and boardrooms of America, and the world.

And what about it?

It begs the question, "what's the difference between the first person and the second?"

And I have a definite answer for you.

The difference between the first person, whose ideas are shot down with little remorse, who people reflexively reject, who fails at an essential component of success, and between the second person, who glides through life with ease, is this: a legacy of credibility.

And that – a long-lasting legacy of complete credibility – is precisely what I'm going to help you develop, in this short volume, if you stick around.

Read the table of contents to prime your mind for what is to come.

Table of Contents

Free $150 Video Course and Bundle of Exclusive Free Bonuses!

All my readers get 12 free bonuses. *You can claim them through the URL on the last page of this book.* Here's what you get:

(1) Free: *The Public Speaking Essential Skills* **video course by the author.** Learn the 20 most important concepts that will immediately simplify public speaking. These 20 concepts will guarantee success as a speaker. They also apply to interpersonal communication between two people or small groups. In this course, I break them each down so that you can instantly (and easily) apply them.

(2) Free: A personal email training with the author after you read. Ask me questions for personalized answers, get speech-writing help, have me edit your speech, send me a video of you speaking for personalized feedback, or even have me help you with your presentation slides. Get access to an expert communication coach for free. Nationally recognized Toastmasters competitors worked with me through this program. They loved the feedback I gave them.

(3) Free: *The Art of Public Speaking,* **by Dale Carnegie.** Learn the crucial principles of public speaking from the author of *How to Win Friends and Influence People.* Discover proven secrets of public speaking that will instantly make you a powerful presence when you speak.

(4) Free: *Public Speaking,* **by Clarence Stratton.** Learn hidden, little-known public speaking secrets from an ivy-league professor. Discover proven methods for quickly and effortlessly defeating public speaking anxiety.

(5) Free: *The Training of a Public Speaker,* **by Grenville Kleiser.** Discover a proven framework for mastering the art of public speaking. Turn yourself from an inexperienced, anxious speaker to an expert, confident one. Do this with the proven wisdom of one of the most respected writers in the field.

(6) Free: *Successful Methods of Public Speaking,* **by Grenville Kleiser.** Discover the proven methods of successful public speakers that are guaranteed to instantly make you a more effective, confident, and persuasive speaker. Learn the exact techniques used by history's great speakers.

(7) Free: Phrases for Public Speakers and Paragraphs for Study, by Grenville Kleiser. Get access to a list of useful phrases designed to improve your speeches. Simply scan the list, identify a useful phrase, and engineer it into your speech for instant eloquence. Get access to a set of excerpts from famous speeches that contain hidden, little-known secrets of public speaking success.

(8) Free: A 29-page book summary of my first book, which includes every chapter. Learn over 500 techniques for expert communication. Use this book summary to instantly remind yourself of what you need to do in your next speech. I simplify each chapter to a short set of bullet-points that will immediately give you the main ideas.

(9) Free: A technique reminder sheet. Every single body language and vocal technique in the entire book *How to Master Public Speaking* summarized in one page. Read it before your next speech to guarantee that you take advantage of these proven principles of persuasive public speaking.

(10) Free: A 208-question self-assessment to help you identify improvements. What are the exact parts of public speaking and persuasive communication where you struggle the most? Find out with this 208-question self-assessment.

(11) Free: A PDF of parts of the book to share with friends. Got a friend or family member who is anxious about an upcoming presentation? Lend them a helping hand by sharing this free PDF of sections from the book *How to Master Public Speaking* and *Effective Communication: the Patterns of Easy Influence.*

(12) Free: A reminder sheet of the entire credibility syntax in this book. Step 1: read this book. Step 2: print out this PDF packet and never forget the powerful persuasive patterns covered in this book. Step 3:

enjoy effortless persuasion. Step 4: give this packet to anyone you want to see succeed, and teach them what you know.

The Basics of Communication Theory: A Quick Summary of the Proven, Must-Know Principles of Compelling Communication that Works

In keeping with my mission of making this book as short and condensed as possible without sacrificing content or quality (to aid the probably very busy people who are reading it), I am going to do something a little different.

I am going to give you a quick list of the foundational principles of communication theory in this section.

Why say something in more words if you can say it in less, right?

In the next three sections, I am going to teach you some basics of effective delivery: in other words, not *what* you say, but *how* you say it.

The focus of this book is speaking with credibility, but that is only a wise goal if you know the basics of effective speaking first.

You must learn to walk before you learn to run.

And if you already know how to walk, then skip these first four sections. But even for you, they are an extremely valuable checklist for compelling communication, and you will probably find something new.

So, let's get into the fundamental theories. If you've read my other books, you are no stranger to these.

Audience characteristic model: every audience is dramatically and meaningfully unique, and you must understand (1) how they are unique, and (2) how you should adjust your communication to tend to that uniqueness. Some unique components of your audiences to consider? Your audience's needs. Your audience's beliefs. Your audience's values. Your audience's objections. Your audience's pain points. Your audience's preconceptions about you. Your audience's value hierarchy. Your audience's past experiences with speakers like you. Your audience's past experiences with ideas like yours. Your audience's experience in similar situations. Your audience's driving desires.

Saliency, intensity, and stability: to get attention when you speak, you must talk about a subject that is relevant to 75% or more of your audience (salient), that these people care strongly about (intensity), and that they will care about for a long time (stability). And, if you cannot, align your subject with something salient, intense, and stable, usually a consequence of your subject.

Benefits: people do things because they benefit them. People don't do things that don't help them. You must convey clear benefits of listening to your communication to your audience, and you must also communicate clear benefits of doing what you want them to do. And benefits for them, not you.

The new, simple, relevant triad: engaging, captivating, and compelling communication is made up of words that convey ideas which are (1) novel to your audience, (2) as simple as they can be, and no simpler, and (3) relevant to your audience.

Psychological persuasion: communication works because it appeals to the psychological characteristics of human cognition; because it plays upon the functions of how human minds work. Communication that accidentally brings psychological forces to bear against the interests of the communicator fails.

Audience desires and WIIFM: compelling communication focuses on helping the audience members (whether they are one person or one hundred) achieve the fundamental things they desire. Compelling communication answers the question, "what's in it for me?" which audience members are always subconsciously thinking.

Structure: the same words in a different sequence can be drastically less potent than those words placed in the correct series. More broadly, there are thousands of macro (whole-communication) and micro (down to sentence-level) communication structures that organize words for maximum impact, usually by satisfying the constraints of many of these other theories.

Ethos, pathos, and logos: the three key principles of rhetoric and persuasion advanced by Aristotle. Ethos is the authority of the speaker, the qualities the audience sees in the speaker; Ethos is the perception that the speaker has the interests of the audience at heart, and the ability to satisfy these interests. Statistics and evidence achieve ethos. Pathos is emotional persuasion that creates the emotion most likely to compel the desired audience action. There must be alignment between the emotion created and the action desired. Emotional stories achieve pathos. Logos is the use of logic to connect central claims to evidence. Intuitive reasoning is a form of logos. The most effective communication uses all three in abundance.

Kairos: almost all schools teach ethos, pathos, and logos, but leave out Kairos. Big mistake. Kairos is timing. Kairos is the impact of what is going on in the real world on your communication. If you are persuading an audience to stop aggressive accounting practices, but Congress just passed a bill sanctioning aggressive accounting practices, Kairos is not in your favor. If Congress publicly committed to ending aggressive accounting practices, Kairos is. The best example is this: if you are trying to persuade the audience to change any status quo, Kairos will be in your favor when that status quo is failing. More on this later.

Emotion and logic: pathos (emotion) completes most persuasion, but first, the audience must have their "logical mind" put to rest by logos (logic) and ethos (evidence), to let their guard down and allow pathos to work its persuasive magic.

Mirroring: human beings psychologically mirror the sentiments portrayed by those communicating with them. If a speaker tells a sad story with sad delivery (sad vocal modulation and body language), the audience mirrors that.

The communication triad: all effective communication successfully (1) connects the communicator(s) to the receiver(s), (2) connects the message(s) to the receiver(s), and (3) connects the message(s) to the communicator(s), in no particular order.

The toolbox triad and your three languages: the communication triad is satisfied with the use of your three languages; your word language (the consciously and subconsciously registered meaning of your words), your vocal language (what is conveyed by your vocal modulation), and your body language (what is conveyed by your body language).

Activation, control, and alignment: to complete the three connections demanded by the communication triad, your three languages must be (1) activated (all in play), (2) controlled (all in your deliberate control), and (3) aligned to one another (all conveying the same meaning). If a speaker is saying confident words with nervous vocal modulation and passive body language, then the three languages are activated, but not controlled and not aligned. Thus, the communication is not effective.

The mental checklist: to decide whether or not to listen to, trust, and work with a speaker, the audience quickly runs through a mental checklist, subconsciously, including questions like "Do I find this speaker trustworthy? Do I have to use too many mental calories to take in this information? Do I have something to gain from this information? Do I have any competing inputs that might be more fruitful? Do I like this speaker? Do I think this speaker knows what I need? Do I think this speaker understands my pain points? Do I think this speaker can be the steward of a valuable solution to a problem in my life? Do I think this information will help me survive and thrive? Do I think this speaker understands me and cares about me? Do I think this speaker is self-motivated and wants to gain something from me? Do I think there's anything in it for me?"

The eight-second cutoff: the audience usually runs through this checklist in eight seconds. Impressions made in the first eight seconds are much harder to overturn later on, though you can.

Substance: effective communication conveys more information with fewer words. A mathematical equation is (1*complete pieces of information + 0.5*repeated pieces of information for the first repetition + 0.5*number of introductory or contextual pieces of information) % (number of words). Maximize the value of this equation to become an efficient communicator.

Inclusivity: one of the most important aspects of a successful speaker to audience connection is inclusivity. The audience must be able to find themselves in the message. They must feel their experiences echoed. For our brief overview, one of the most compelling examples is using inclusive pronouns, like saying, "We all struggle because of this problem," instead of "you all struggle because of this problem."

Medicine: in most communication situations, you are proposing a solution to a problem. You are selling medicine to a sickness, and the medicine (the solution) only makes sense in the context of the sickness (the problem) it solves. Don't just propose solutions; talk about the problems they solve.

Empathy and authority: the most compelling speakers portray two qualities. They portray empathy ("I feel your pain and understand the struggles you face") and authority ("Here are the credentials that prove that I can solve the struggles and ease the pain.")

The people's pain: more broadly than empathy and authority, people have problems that cause pain, and effective communicators talk about the problems, the pain they produce, and the solutions that can solve the problems and ease the pain.

What and how: communication is not only powerful because of what is said, but how it is said. A strong message (the what) spoken weakly (the how) appears weak, not strong.

Purposeful communication: communication must have a purpose; else, you should not even attempt it. And, every single use of the three languages in communication must either (1) contribute to the purpose of the communication, or (2) be removed. This does not mean "business only" communication. For example, if you are trying to persuade someone to do something, this doesn't mean that you have only to hammer them with information about the proposal. Speaking briefly about something humorous or personable is indeed purposeful communication because it fosters likeability, and likable people are more persuasive.

Cone of attention: every single audience, based on their characteristics, has a set of subjects that, if spoken about, will cause them to narrow their focus to only the communicator. The cone broadens; at the opposite end, are subjects and messages that receive no attention (the cone is broad and includes more things other than the speaker), and in the middle, there is some attention. Try to stay at the top of the cone (where it narrows to a point, only including you and nothing else) by understanding your audience, what interests them, and what they want.

Conscious and subconscious: communication occurs at both a conscious and subconscious level. Truly impactful persuasion appeals to both conscious and subconscious psychology, moderately effective persuasion appeals to only the conscious mind, and failed communication appeals to neither. This is a big theory with big implications, and my promise for this overview was brevity, so I will give you a quick example. When you are speaking, there are specific vocal tonalities that create subconscious impressions in your audience's minds. This simply means that they could not consciously point out the causes (these tonalities) and the effects (how they change audience cognition), but that these causes (the tonalities) are so subtle that the effects (the impressions they cause) occur below the awareness of the audience's conscious minds.

Perceived net gain: in extended form, the equation is perceived marginal gain minus perceived marginal cost. Your audience is continually running through a mental loop that is asking them if perceived marginal gain (what they get from your communication and offer) is greater than perceived marginal cost (the mental resources they use to listen and the resources they give up for your offer, like money and time). They particularly do this in two places: (1) at the start of communication ("what do I get from listening, what do I have to give up, and is this a sufficiently positive transaction of attention for me?") and (2) when evaluating any offers ("what do I get from doing what this speaker wants, what do I have to give up, and is this a sufficiently positive transaction for me?") The more positive their perceived net gain is, the more attention you get. If it becomes negative, the audience checks out. Note that this is perceived net gain, not actual net gain: it's what the audience *thinks* they gain or lose, and how much they value that. Balance this equation in your favor by creating the perception (and indeed, the reality) of higher gain and lower costs from your communication and your offer. Some people demand an extremely high net gain to exchange mental resources (to pay attention) or physical resources (to spend money). In contrast, other people just want to see a moderately positive transaction. And remember this: the more positive the equation, the more attention you get. It's a spectrum, not a switch.

The wind and the sun: this is one of Aesop's fables. The moral is that gentle, subtle, and strategic persuasion and communication is more influential than aggressive, coercive communication. The wind and sun wanted to get a traveler's coat off. The wind blew and blew and blew, but the traveler just pulled his coat tighter. The wind's violent gusts represent aggressive, "hard-sell" tactics. But the sun shined its warm beams on the traveler, and he took the coat off on his own. The traveler taking off his jacket illustrates another moral: you cannot convince anyone. You cannot control their minds. They must convince themselves, and you must provide the ingredients and incentives for them to do so. You must create a gentle, slippery slope that causes them to convince themselves. This is the only way. You can never tear anyone's coat off. You can only get them to take it off themselves.

Mental malleability: certain mental states are most conducive to your communication fulfilling its goals. Just what mental states are most important depends on your goals. Still, some constants are (1) attention, (2) a connection to the communicator, (3) a connection to the message,

(4) emotional certainty in the offer or proposal, and (5) logical certainty in the offer or proposal. Mental malleability states that your communication inputs can change your audience's mental states and that effective communication does so in your favor.

Spectrums: we can identify mental states as one through ten spectrums, where a one is "does not possess this quality," and a ten is "fully possesses this quality." This is a useful mental model. Identify the qualities of the mental state most conducive to your communication fulfilling its goals, break it down into a set of spectrums, and use mental malleability to edge your audience from ones to tens. For example, the mental state for a politician seeking to convert independent voters to one of the major parties should include as one of its qualities "anger towards the other party." Thus, the speaker should work towards raising the audience from a one to a ten on this spectrum of anger towards the other party.

One versus many: I will never, ever tell you that these strategies are guaranteed to work, because of one reason and one reason only: external variables are incredibly hyperactive in complex situations, such as communication. In other words, I can tell you that strategy X produces impact Y on your audience, and know that with scientifically backed certainty. However, I cannot tell you that there will not be 200 other variables in play working against impact Y.

Ceteris paribus: ceteris paribus is Latin for "all else equal." And these strategies demand the ceteris paribus assumption: that you isolate the relationship between a cause (a speaking strategy) and its impact (the impression created in the mind of the audience). I guarantee that *ceteris paribus*, these strategies will work in your favor. I do not guarantee that these strategies will automatically work. Why? Because I do not know what negative variables are at play. Nor do I know how strong they are, or how numerous. And I do not know whether or not they wipe out the positive impacts of a strategy. What I will tell you is this: based on my experience, on the science behind many of these strategies, and on the people I have consulted (including my readers, my students, and other writers about this subject), these strategies almost always wipe out the negative impacts of external variables. But I refuse to guarantee something will *always* happen if it only *almost always* happens.

Certainty: the certainty principle is that people are inherently inert and inherently averse to risk, and thus must be entirely confident before taking action. This already seems straightforward. But apply the spectrum model to certainty, and see how simple it becomes. Take the people from a one certainty level to a ten certainty level. Jordan Belfort, a famous sales coach, bolstered my understanding of this principle. He teaches that there are two kinds of certainty: emotional certainty ("I feel good about this") and logical certainty ("I think this is a good idea"). He also states that all objections to an idea are often smokescreens for uncertainty.

Counterfactual simulation: when people are considering how to act, what plan to select, or what path to follow, they automatically perform counterfactual simulation. Counterfactual simulation is when they play out the course of events ensuing from an action, and determine, based on this mental movie, whether or not to take that action. They direct a mental movie of the events that will ensue after they do (or don't do something), which will help them decide whether to do (or not do) it. Skeptics, people who often don't believe something despite strong evidence in its favor, often tend to produce unrealistically negative counterfactual simulations. Credibility means that when someone is deciding whether they should (1) listen to you, and (2) do what you suggest, they have overwhelmingly positive counterfactual simulations. They paint a positive mental movie of listening to you and following your suggestion because you have a legacy of credibility and because you are speaking in specific ways, which we'll talk about in this book. :)

Contrasts: contrasts between two things are infinitely more potent in human information interpretation than any of the two items on their own. For example, when you are persuading others to choose between two paths, do not only highlight the benefits of path one. You must also highlight the detriments of path two. Why? Because people much more easily interpret the contrast between the two than either of the two on their own. And not only is it easier, but much more impactful. "Path A is good" is weaker than "Path A is good, and path B is bad."

Sequence: the same words, arranged in a different sequence, take on an entirely new power if sequenced properly. The art of communication structure is the art of understanding such sequence effects, and incorporating them into simple formulas.

Frames: all communication deals with frames. A frame is a relationship between two things. "X [insert relationship] Y." For example: "This policy is bad," where X is the policy, the relationship is an equivalency, and Y is the quality "bad." This seems extremely elementary, but drastically underestimated and dramatically powerful frame-effects occur in specific kinds of reframing. Reframing is the art of taking a frame and changing it (as in a debate or argument), and there are dozens of specific ways of changing the frame that are particularly powerful. A relationship reversal is one of these specific, sophisticated reframes. You keep the X and the Y, but take the relationship and turn it into its opposite. For example, if the first frame is "X contradicts Y," you take the relationship ("contradicts") and invert it while keeping X and Y the same: "X is true because of Y," or a functional equivalent, "X justifies Y." The relationship reversal is one of just many extremely compelling reframing effects. We'll cover these in greater depth in the final chapter.

Aspirations: everyone has hopes and appealing to these aspirations and aspirational identities is a powerful strategy for persuading action.

Unspoken words: certain communication strategies implicitly and subconsciously impart meanings that you could not literally say. The audience, in a way, hears unspoken words. For example, using (1) the "APP method" (where you open communication by agreeing to a common struggle, promising a solution, and previewing the solution), (2) open body language (where you completely open your torso to the audience and use outward gestures), and (3) an empathetic vocal tonality, subconsciously imparts the words "Trust me! I have empathy for you! Here's your problem, which is what I'm trying to sell you a solution to. I promise that this solution is worth-your-while! You should be curious about it. Be curious this instant!" You could never, under any circumstances, say these words out loud. But they are understood implicitly and subconsciously, and for this reason, they have a positive effect.

Loss aversion: people are risk-averse, and feel the pain from a loss (-$1,000) more than they feel the pleasure from an equivalent gain (+$1,000). Some people feel the loss twice as much. -$1,000 has a negative emotional impact that is equivalent in magnitude to the positive emotional impact of +$2,000. This means that the best benefits are not only a gain but protection from some loss or risk of loss. In other words, "this plan is the best because it will raise our profitability by 20%" is inferior to "this plan is the best because it will raise our profitability by 20% while nearly entirely eradicating the risk of sinking share value."

Persuasion aversion: the fable of the wind and the sun teach us that people do not want to see themselves as being persuaded. People seek internal consistency. Letting you convince them to do something that they haven't done before makes them feel inconsistent. Them doing it now would be inconsistent with them not having done it so far. This is one of the principal sources of persuasion aversion, in addition to loss and risk aversion, and the belief that someone always gets the short end of the stick, and that it must be them if you are trying to get them to do something. Otherwise, if you were getting the short end, why try to get them on board?

Purpose statements and transitions: all competent, purposeful communication is made up of purpose statements (statements that are strategically and deliberately designed to advance the overall goal of the communication), and transitions (connections between the purpose statements that hold attention and create fluidity and flow). Also, all competent, purposeful communication includes little of anything else.

The transparency fallacy: communicators far too often believe that their audience knows what is going on in their heads; that they are transparent. A nervous speaker assumes that the audience will know that. This is not the case. The audience only forms impressions based on external inputs. This is why the "fake confidence" strategy works: the audience knows no better, despite the feeling that your inner thoughts are there for everyone to see.

The evolved mind: all effective communication does one thing, broken up into three parts. Those three parts are these: (1) brings to bear psychological forces in the minds of the audience to (2) get them to do something beneficial to the communicator and (3) favorable to themselves. How did those psychological forces get there? Through genetic and cultural evolution. And since genetic and cultural evolution has sculpted the human mind, the keys to the lock of human psychology (and thus effective communication) are to be found in our evolutionary history. This will likely be the subject of an entire book I'll write later on.

Cognitive load: audiences have a fixed amount of mental resources. Effective speakers know how to budget these mental resources and how to limit the cognitive load. If the cognitive load exceeds the benefits of the communication (the mental resources they lose by listening exceed what they gain by listening), they check out. The best communicators keep cognitive load as low as possible, but no lower.

And this final theory is terrific.

Truly wonderful.

Why?

Because it is a treasure that will revolutionize your career.

It's called the credibility cascade.

The credibility cascade: there is a logical fallacy called the "ad hominem" or "at the person." For example, this occurs in a debate when one person attacks the opposition's character, instead of the ideas the opposition advanced. While it is a logical fallacy, it tells us something important about human psychology and cognition: the source of the message matters more than it logically should. The fact that it is such an emphasized logical fallacy tells us something. It tells us that an extremely common characteristic of human psychology is to substitute the easy question of "what do I think of the source of the message?" for the harder question of "what do I think of the message itself?" And why does this happen? Think about cognitive load. Substituting the easy question conserves cognitive resources. Our brains are lazy. And this is the reason why that first person in the boardroom got nowhere, while the second did, despite almost identical messages. Because the source matters. So, this is the credibility cascade: you are neutral at first, and then you communicate credibly once. Twice. Three times. What happens? You gain a reputation for credibility. Not only are you credible because you are speaking credibly in the moment, but because you have done so countless times in the past. This is a positive feedback loop, self-reinforcing snowball effect. You now have the weight of not only your credible communication in any particular instance, but the weight of your credible reputation produced by all the times you have communicated credibly in the past. Every piece of credible communication does two things: first, it takes effect in the moment, but second, it places an investment into a bank account of credibility that will compound over time, getting people to place massive trust in you instantly. Why? Because the source of the message matters more than it should.

Your Three Languages: How to Instantly Simplify Communication in Your Career by Understanding One Easy Concept

You know you have three languages. And now, I am going to give you the five most important tools for empowering each before we get into the art of credibility. All effective communication is masterfully using your three languages, by understanding a simple set of speaking strategies. Remember: before you learn how to speak with credibility, you must build a foundation of firm basics: voice projection, eye contact, straightforward sentences, etc. Without those, you will lack engagement, poise, and command of your communication. And without *those*, you will not be able to communicate credibly. Let's get into the strategies.

Your Word Language Basics: How to Master the Simple, Step-by-Step Basic Strategies for Clear, Compelling and Captivating Words

Strategy #1, the hook opening: start your communication with an opening designed to hook the attention of the audience. The APP model is one of the thousands of models I've developed. Another one is the "if benefit(s), minus risk(s), then action" opening: "if we want [insert benefit one], [insert benefit two], and [insert benefit three], without the risk of [insert loss], then we should [insert action]." Another is the past, present, means: "(Past problems) In my last company, we had six consecutive quarters of declining capitalization, without even making long-term capital investments. Shareholders were up in arms, the press was vicious, and there was a general panic at the offices. (Present successes) Now, we have had six consecutive quarters of positive growth, exceeding our previous peak. The Financial Daily magazine gave us the most-promising-stock reward. Everyone was back on track. (Means of transition) How did we do that? When they promoted me to tier two management, I did three things: I shed costly investments without mercilessly laying off labor, and I also reinstated discipline with a scientifically proven incentive structure. Most importantly, I corrected accounting lapses without succumbing to the allure of aggressive and dishonest accounting. I believe the qualities that let me turn around that company will be instrumental in designing a positive future for this one."

Strategy #2, call to action: since all worth-while communication is purposeful, and since that purpose is often to get people to do something, calls to action are instrumental. After you have persuaded them, tell them what to do. And make sure that, right before you do that, you do three things: raise the perceived benefit of acting, lower the perceived cost of acting, and request a specific action.

Strategy #3, Cialdini's six persuasive methods: Robert Cialdini of the University of Arizona is a genius. In his groundbreaking book, *Influence: The Psychology of Persuasion*, he advances six persuasive principles. Likeability: people are persuaded by those they like. Scarcity: people want what is scarce. Reciprocity: people are persuaded by those who have done something for them. Authority: people are persuaded by authority figures. Consensus or social proof: people are persuaded by the actions of other people, and often go with the crowd. Consistency: people are persuaded to act in ways consistent with their previous actions.

Strategy #4, rhetorical questions: rhetorical questions engage people and function as transitions. Use them often to keep attention. After making a declaratory statement of fact, and you want to analyze it, use a rhetorical question transition by, for example, saying, "But what exactly does this mean for us?" In other words, ask the rhetorical question you are about to answer.

Strategy #5, stories: a significant clue to the biases and systematic errors made by human psychology is the list of logical fallacies. A logical fallacy is probably emphasized as a logical fallacy because lots of people make it. And one of the logical fallacies that gets the most attention is the "anecdotal fallacy," wherein people extrapolate a general rule based on one anecdote. What does this teach us? That people are prone to extrapolate general rules based on anecdotes and stories. Otherwise, it wouldn't be one of the most commonly taught logical fallacies. So, while you should always support your positions with statistics and empirical evidence, anecdotal examples told as stories are often more effective. Use both.

Your Voice Language Basics: How to Master the Fundamental Foundations of Energetic and Engaging Vocal Modulation

Strategy #1, tone and tonality: you've probably heard the word "tone" so many times, usually attached to vague pieces of advice about how to do it. Let me simplify it once and for all. As you know, your three languages must be in alignment. And that means that the way your voice sounds must match the sentiment of your words. Are your words an intellectual analysis of something? Then your vocal tone should be analytical and rational. So, how do you achieve this? Apply this thought-experiment, which I call the "through-the-wall experiment:" pretend that there was someone in the other room, listening to you speak. Pretend that they couldn't hear your exact words, but only the sound of your voice. How would they say you sounded? That would be your tone. Let's say you are happily praising someone with your words, but the "through-the-wall experiment" tells you that the eavesdropper would say you were angrily criticizing someone. That would be a problem.

Strategy #2, vocal projection: you know you must project your voice. You obviously understand that your voice must be loud enough to be heard by voice listeners. But what if you have a naturally quiet voice? Then, do three things. First, take a deep breath, until your diaphragm comfortably expands, and speak as you release the air. Second, try to speak from the mask of your face, or the area that a surgical mask would cover. You should feel this area vibrating as you speak. Third, pretend you are having a conversation with the person in the room who is furthest from you.

Strategy #3, PPP variation: do not be monotone. Do not put your listeners to sleep, and eliminate the efficacy of your vocal language with monotony. Always vary your voice. But how? By playing with three levers; the PPP levers, your projection, your pace, and your pitch. And while random variation of your PPP qualities is better than monotony, strategic PPP variation is better than random variation. What's strategic variation? It simply means modulating your PPP qualities to achieve the desired impression. Indeed, this is how you would achieve your tone. For example, want to portray passion and intensity? Raise your projection, raise your pace, and raise your pitch. Want to portray confidence and calm control? Moderately raise your projection, lower your pace, and lower your pitch. You are, at this point, speaking somewhat loudly, but with a slower and more controlled pace than before, and with a deeper, booming pitch. See how that creates the desired impression?

Strategy #4, breaking rapport and opening rapport: within the infinite variety of pitch modulations are two that deserve special attention. Breaking rapport is when your pitch goes down at the end of your sentence. Opening rapport is when your pitch goes up at the end of your sentence. Breaking rapport creates the impression of confidence, conclusion, and credibility; that what you are saying is confirmed, stands on its own, and needs no external validation. Opening rapport, also known as question rapport, indicates just that: that what you are saying demands validation, like how a question demands validation from an answer. But when someone asks you a question, you instantly perk up and give them attention. And you often know it's a question only because of this tonality. So this tonality has the benefit of grabbing attention. But how do you use these tonalities? Use opening rapport on statements for which your conviction is unquestionable. For example, your personal introduction is such a statement. This draws people in but doesn't make you seem unsure, as this tonality does typically. Why? Because obviously, you know your personal introductory information. Now, what about substantive statements, for which you want to seem credible? That's when you use breaking rapport. Never, ever, under any circumstances, make a substantive, declaratory statement that is relevant to your purpose, with question tonality. That will completely undermine your credibility. But that doesn't happen with statements where your confidence is unquestionable.

Strategy #5, pausing: words might be eloquent, but no word has ever been as fluent as a correctly timed pause. Pauses grab attention, build intrigue, raise suspense, and create natural eloquence. Also, they give you time to formulate your next sentence in the best possible way. Watch a video of Barack Obama speaking, and you'll see the power of pausing as a speaking strategy.

Your Body Language Basics: How to Master the Basics of Body Language that Conveys Confidence and Portrays Poise

Strategy #1, planted feet: the vast majority of people will make a crucial mistake when speaking from a standing position. They will do something weird with their feet and weight distribution. Either they will tap their feet or, more commonly, shift their weight from foot to foot. You don't want to look like a palm tree in a monsoon, do you? When has a palm tree blowing around in a hurricane ever appeared credible to you? Plant your feet firmly to the ground, and if you move, move with purpose; a controlled, smooth, suave pace from one position to another, not an erratic shift in your weight.

Strategy #2, eye contact: you must make eye contact with your listeners. The common objection is, "But Peter, I'm reading information from a manuscript in front of me... how do I make eye contact?" My first response is that people want to hear you speak directly to them. They do not want to see you look at a manuscript, get the information, and then give it to them. So, limit the words on your visual aids to short phrases, which allows you to deliver a smooth stream of consciousness. My second response is this: read your information, then look up, and deliver it while making eye contact.

Strategy #3, open posture: closed posture (receded position, leaning back, with the palms of your hands hidden away, and with your arms crossed over your chest) communicates insecurity and anxiety. Those are not credible qualities. Open posture (engaged, upright position with good posture, leaning forward, with palms facing the audience and gesturing by your sides, with a smile, with your head held high, with outward gestures, and with an open torso) communicates confidence, control, and amicability. Those are credible qualities.

Strategy #4, reflexive gestures: you have three languages, and they must be aligned, or saying the same things. You know that. But you might be wondering how to align your body language to your words. And the answer is with reflexive gestures: gestures that reflect the meaning of your words. For example, if your words are describing something vast, a wide, sweeping gesture with your hand will reflect that meaning. Something small? Pinching together your fingers as though you were holding a thumb-tack will reflect that. Get it?

Strategy #5, facial expressions: facial expressions are another lever for aligning your body language to your word language. It's simple: create facial expressions that match the sentiment of your words. And don't fabricate them, unless you have an actor-like ability to manipulate your facial appearance. Just let the emotions you already have about the subject of your words show themselves. That way, you achieve authenticity.

Now That You Know the Basics...

Let me tell you something. And this is under the assumption that you use what you learned. After reading the basic principles of communication theory, you became better than 70% of others at communication. After reading the five word-language strategies, you bumped that up to 80%. After reading the vocal-language strategies? 90%. And after finishing up the body-language strategies, you became better than about 99% of others at the basic principles of communication theory and communication delivery.

But that's not why you came here.

It was just a necessary detour.

Now, we are going to turn you into the most *credible* communicator you can be; more credible than 99% of other people you will encounter along the course of your career.

Let's get into it, my friend.

The Fluency and Magnitude Matrix: How to Present Supporting Evidence in the Most Credible and Compelling Way Possible

Alright. This is where it gets serious. This is where we break down credible communication into a scientifically proven set of predictable principles.

And the first one is the fluency and magnitude matrix.

Let me explain.

Credibility is the art of earning trust and belief.

And how do you earn trust and belief?

By expressing a compelling cache of expert knowledge.

So, let's back up. How do people judge the quality and quantity of *their own* knowledge on a given subject?

Fluency and magnitude.

In other words, when people try to answer a question, let's say, "how many of the president's policies do you know?" they judge the strength of their knowledge of the president's policies on fluency and magnitude.

What does that mean? They judge their comprehension by the fluency with which they remember the president's policies, and the magnitude, or the number of the president's policies that they remember.

Get it? Fluency and magnitude.

And fluency holds more weight than magnitude.

If they quickly and thoroughly – or fluently – remember two policies, they have checked the fluency box, and they judge their knowledge to be reasonably robust. Why not *very* strong? Because they still lack a magnitude of examples.

If they do not quickly remember any policies, but sit down and manage to brainstorm twenty policies over five hours – or a magnitude – then they judge themselves as less competent on this subject than they did when they portrayed fluency, but not magnitude.

And fluency is not always easy. This is why it is such a potent litmus test of subject-area competency. Think about it: why do people say "name three examples" when accused of bad behavior? Because fluency is difficult, and there is a fairly good chance that the accuser will not be able to fluently riff off three examples of the bad behavior, even if they could think of thirty over a more extended time.

Makes sense so far?

And now, let's explore what this has to do with portraying immense credibility to others.

People judge their own subject-area or knowledge-area competency based on the fluency and magnitude with which they respond to a related query.

But it's time for the kicker.

They will also judge *your* subject-area or knowledge-area competency – a key component of credibility – based on your fluency and magnitude of communication.

And that's the secret.

So, how do you make yourself instantly credible, in an impressive way?

Be prepared to portray immense fluency and magnitude in support of your claims and positions.

What's one way to do this? With examples. And examples are, in and of themselves, credibility boosters.

So, make a claim and then fluently rattle off a large magnitude of examples.

But how do you actually deliver fluency? Simply by speaking in a fast, unlabored, easy, and effortless way. Simply by streaming out, without error or complication, a quick barrage of supporting examples. The speed and ease with which you rattle off the examples express your fluency, which bolsters your credibility. And don't make the mistake of picking one example and diving deep into it. There's time for that later. When you want to express fluency, just skim across the surface, like a jet-ski; don't go for a deep-dive just yet.

And how do you deliver magnitude? Simply by continuing until ten or so examples. That's a general rule; that ten examples suffice as a magnitude. It depends on your circumstances. Just keep going until you have achieved what is considered a high magnitude of content for your particular circumstances. That is your subject, your audience, your position, your claim, etc.

So, how do you do this if you don't trust your ability to fluently remember so many examples? It's easy: just write them down in front of you, and read three or so examples with a quick glance down, delivering them fluently after looking back up to achieve eye contact. Or, just practice it to memory. After all, it is just a list of ten or so short phrases.

This is most effective when the units in the list (the number of units in the list being its magnitude) are short phrases.

For example, I gave a speech in college about why the world was getting much, much better. I said, "virtually every measure of human prosperity has drastically improved over time." And then I rattled off the ten examples fluently (I had them on paper). This is the critical part: the examples were just prosperity-measures that improved, meaning that they were one or two-word phrases. For example, "democratic values," or "consumer surplus."

Why is that so important? Because it is easier to fluently rattle-off single word examples, and because magnitude is not *length*, but *number*. If you have one example, and fluently describe that one example for a long duration, that is not magnitude. It is still just one example. You must not emphasize your fluency and magnitude in your knowledge of one specific example, but your knowledge of many examples. This is how the weight of your fluency and magnitude will lend you immense credibility.

What's another way to use this, though?

It's one of my favorites.

It leaves people agape in impressed surprise.

It's a mic-drop moment.

Let's say you anticipate a pointed question or a predictable objection. For example, let's say you are a conservative political pundit, speaking on liberal college campuses, and a politically left-leaning student extolls the virtues of socialism.

Anticipate that.

Have at the ready a response that goes something like this: "Nearly every single Socialist country failed, costing lives, resources, and causing dramatic destruction and destitution *(claim, which will be made more credible with a fluently delivered magnitude of examples, where the examples are short phrases and thus easiest to work into this strategy)*. The Soviet Union failed. Serbia failed. Croatia failed. Slovenia failed. Romania failed. Poland failed. Hungary failed. Angola failed. Ethiopia failed. East Germany failed. Mozambique failed."

See how there are two elements of easy fluency and magnitude? That is, first, a claim where the examples are short phrases (which are easiest to be fluent in), and the ensuing magnitude of those examples, fluently delivered?

Another example of such a pointed question or objection to the conservative pundit is "Capitalist countries produce terrible consequences." The counter-claim from the pundit would be something like, "Capitalist countries produce tremendous benefits. Higher consumer surplus. Higher protection of human rights. Higher protection of fundamental liberties. Nearly 80% of all corporate profit going to labor. Self-interest directed to the betterment of the public. Innovation. Longer life expectancy. Greater measures of self-reported happiness.

More emancipative values. Lower poverty and extreme poverty. Lower rates of starvation. Lower levels of sickness and malnourishment."

See, again, how there are two parts to this? The claim which lends itself to short-phrase examples? And then the magnitude of examples fluently delivered?

I'll repeat it one more time: short-phrase examples are easiest to be fluent in and to deliver a magnitude of quickly.

I use the example of a conservative pundit because hearing one is when I first realized the power of the fluency and magnitude matrix.

Virtually every single instance of the fluency and magnitude matrix in action created a chorus of applause.

Virtually every single instance of the fluency and magnitude matrix in action went viral on social media.

Virtually every single instance of the fluency and magnitude matrix in action crumbled the opposition under the massive weight of perceived credibility the speaker gained.

It is a verbal kill shot that instantly boosts your credibility to massive, unprecedented levels. And I emphasize this word in particular: *instantly*.

It is so fast.

Another quick note: try to make the examples as specific as possible. Humans have a precision bias, which we'll talk about later.

Alright. We are almost done with this one.

Let's cover one more technique for the more sinister among you.

How do you make others seem not-so-credible? They haven't read this book, and you have, so they will not be prepared to demonstrate fluency and magnitude. Portray their lack of fluency and magnitude by asking them a question with a few characteristics.

The first characteristic: it prompts them clearly and unequivocally to support their claim with examples.

The second characteristic: it specifically requests a relatively high magnitude of examples. Magnitude has another function. When there is an anchor magnitude, which people do not question as the accepted burden of proof, if the speaker doesn't reach that anchor magnitude, their credibility is undermined. For example, if you say "give us three examples of…" and they give you three examples, they have boosted their credibility because they met the magnitude level that was accepted (without question) as the necessary proof-threshold. But let's say that you say "give us five examples of…" and they give you three examples. It is literally the same amount of proof as when you asked for three examples, but it does not meet your magnitude anchor, which was unquestioned as the threshold of proof. The impact? They do not have perceived magnitude, and they have much less perceived credibility, even though the proof is literally identical. But it will be questioned if you push it too far. If you ask for twenty examples, that's a little ridiculous. Keep it higher than what you think they can provide, and lower than what will expose the strategy.

The third characteristic: it is not too insulting, derisive, or confrontational. That makes you seem unobjective and personally involved and actually hurts your credibility. Pleasantries must precede it. For example: "I'm actually of a different opinion, but I recognize that I could be wrong. I trust you, and you'll persuade me if you can give me [insert number] of examples." Or, "I definitely see where you're coming from. It makes sense. I'm not opposed to that. But can you give us [insert number of examples]? That would push me over the edge."

The fourth characteristic: sprinkle ease phrases around your request of examples, which serve to imply that giving the examples should be fluent. For example: "can you *just quickly* give us a *few short, simple* examples? Maybe [insert anchor magnitude]?"

The fifth characteristic: ask a question for which a fluent response is inherently tricky. In other words, ask a question which (1) you think the receiver is not prepared to answer, (2) by its nature does not lend itself to examples which are short phrases, and instead (3) demands longer, complex examples. I can't tell you what this magic question will be, and I suggest giving it some thought. It depends on your circumstances, such as your subject of discussion, and the subject-knowledge of the other person.

And let's say this works like a charm, and they don't use the fluency-magnitude matrix because it is not natural to them.

Jump in with your opposing viewpoint, and ace the fluency-magnitude matrix, just like I taught you. Say the opposite claim, and the fluent magnitude of examples you have neatly prepared.

They'll hate you for it, but you'll be seen as credible by everyone else in the room, and they'll get over it, and you'll advance.

It works like a charm. :)

Intuitive Bias: How to Modulate Your Delivery to Appeal to a Hidden Component of Human Cognition and Psychology

This one is simple. But extremely effective, despite being so easy to use.

And for a few decades, only Republican politicians understood it and used it. This is a big reason why some of them had such tremendous success going up against their Democrat counterparts who not only didn't use it but accidentally went against it.

But what exactly is it?

What is the intuitive bias?

And, most importantly, how can we use it to be more credible in our everyday communication?

These are all critical questions, which I will answer shortly.

But first, we must address an even more fundamental question.

What even is a bias?

Let me tell you. A bias is a systematic cognitive shortcut that, while often helpful in conserving mental resources, inadvertently and secretly creates many misjudgments.

In simpler terms: bias is a systematic mental function that causes thinking mistakes and is baked right into our psychology, probably because it gave us some evolutionary advantage at some point in the history of our species.

Think about it: biases often lead to snap judgments, and snap judgments were very advantageous 2,000 years ago. For example: "that thing has big teeth, I'm going to head out now."

But, what about this bias, in particular?

This is what our intuitive bias means: we find intuitive, simple, easily understood explanations, proposals, and positions, much more credible than complex, convoluted, and confusing ones with high cognitive load.

In simpler terms: simpler is better (see what I did there?) because it is more credible.

And how can we use it?

Always reduce.

Always simplify.

Always avoid unnecessary complexity.

And let's talk about this last one: avoid *unnecessary* complexity, not *all* complexity. Make it as simple as it can be, but no simpler.

You should expect that when I teach you something like the intuitive bias, I don't just flat-out tell you to avoid complexity, and leave it at that. You should expect that when I teach you *any* component of human psychology, I don't just give you one tool to make it work in your favor, but many.

That said, the reduce, simplify, and avoid unnecessary complexity triad is the most fundamental of these tools. Don't even bother using any of the others until you get this one down.

So, what are the other tools?

Use simple equivalencies. Simple equivalencies are sticky. They are memorable, and they are summative; they are easy to remember and contain the fundamentals of your message in them. For example: "X is just plain wrong and immoral." Or, "X is not what America stands for." Or, "X is simply where the evidence leads." See what I mean? The basic form is "X is Y."

Use sententia. Sententia is a rhetorical device of aesthetic form (which we will discuss later when we talk about the aesthetic impact bias). All you have to do to use sententia is to summarize a previous, complex unit of meaning (such as a paragraph, structural segment, or long sentence) in a simple, eloquent, memorable way. For example, after a particularly information-heavy, complicated and non-intuitive explanation of how a politician's policies will help a constituency, a solid use of sententia would be something like "a vote for me is a vote for the future of this community." This is effective because it doesn't force you to cut anything in the pursuit of intuitive communication, and because the complicated explanation validates the sententia. If you just said "a vote for me is a vote for the future of this community," it would be invalid. It would fall flat. It just wouldn't work. But not so after the longer explanation. See how these strategies kill not only two, but a handful of birds, with one stone? See how they are mutually interdependent and empowering as they act in an interconnected web?

Use reframing effects. I touched on reframing effects previously. Let me elaborate. Here's what reframing is: changing the relationship between the two subjects. (Actually, it's a bit more complicated. This is just basic reframing). For example, here are some logical relationships: X causes Y, X happens because of Y, X happens despite Y, X is necessary for Y, X is disconnected from Y, X contradicts Y. And here's what frame escalation is: zooming out on a common frame and reversing it from a new perspective. It is changing the perceived relationship between two things. It is controlling the narrative and the information. For example: let's say most people criticize a public figure. They say X statement from the person contradicts Y statement from the person. If you disagree, there are a few options: you could say the contradiction doesn't matter or find a way to say it isn't a contradiction. But there's one excellent option: escalating the frame from an "X contradicts Y" statement, to an "X is true because of Y" statement. This is so insanely counterintuitive but powerful. The world's most effective politicians, and the winners of political debates, have been the ones who have used frame escalation. Frame escalation is especially effective if the new frame and the original frame seem to be at odds with one another. In other words: frame escalation is particularly powerful, persuasive, and elegant if the new frame seems to undo or completely reverse the old frame while maintaining the original X and Y.

Use numbers and stories. Numbers provide information but not persuasion, and stories provide persuasion but not information. Well, that's not entirely true. Numbers provide some persuasion, and stories provide some information, but by and large, the original assertion remains correct. Why, though? Here's why: because the human mind is not great at comprehending numbers, but extremely adept at interpreting stories. The standard story structure is a vehicle for transferring information that has passed down information (like the fable of the wind and the sun) from generation to generation, over thousands of years. We are so good at interpreting stories that we often make them up to simplify our understanding of the world, even if there is no legitimate story to be told. So, by all means, go ahead and use numbers. Numbers are extremely credible as quantitative proof. But to get some real impact, describe a story that is an example of the truth you want to convey with the numbers. For example, Bernie Sanders often lists statistics of income inequality. That's only bad because he doesn't proceed to give his audiences some stories about how those numbers take effect in the lives of Americans. Stories are intuitive.

Use buzzwords. Buzzwords are big, bold, intuitive concepts that diffuse easily. What do I mean by that? I mean that they are so simple, so impactful, and so potent that people talk about them. And they *can* talk about them because they are easy and simple. A buzzword is like a big banner with one word or short phrase on it, that acts as an umbrella, containing your complex message under it. These are examples of political buzzwords: equality, opportunity, freedom. And here are some business buzzwords: innovation, shareholder value, profit. So, how do you use these intuitive buzzwords to apply the intuitive bias in your favor? By connecting a simple, generally agreeable buzzword to your complex message. Let's say you wanted to post a social media picture describing your message. The caption would be the complex message, and what you would use as your hashtags would represent your buzzwords. It's the same relationship. (I apologize if this social media metaphor is alien to you).

Use values. Evoking values is one of the most common communication techniques of the world's shakers and movers. And it works. People love their values. Values are a form of buzzwords. Where do they differ from buzzwords? Values are, essentially, favored virtues. Buzzwords are not. Just like all penguins are birds, but not all birds are penguins, all values are buzzwords, but not all buzzwords are values. For example, in the Trump administration, "the wall" is a buzzword, but it is not a value. The corresponding value would probably be "national sovereignty." Attach complex, high cognitive-load communication, to simple, generally agreeable values.

Use visualization. We are visual creatures. We interpret visual information much faster than non-visual information. Tell them not only what it *is*, but how it *looks*. If you were going to film a movie of a sentence, where would you point your camera? That's the visual component that you should use to activate the intuitive bias in your favor. And, even better, is this: use visual data. Print out sheets of paper with visualized data (charts and graphs) that illustrate the numerical evidence you are bringing to the table. Why? Again, because we interpret it significantly better in visual form. For example, if your evidence is the growing gap between two measurements, the numerical gap is far, far less intuitive than the visual gap on a line graph of the two measurements over time.

Use analogies, metaphors, and similes. An analogy is describing an unfamiliar situation (what you are describing) to an intuitive, familiar situation. A metaphor is using non-literal comparison to draw a similarity between one thing and another. A simile is a metaphor that uses the words like or as. An analogy: "nightfall is like drawing a curtain because [describe similarities]. A metaphor: "the curtain of nightfall fell." A simile: "like a curtain, nightfall fell." Now, why do this at all? Well, it's only worth doing if you are comparing an unfamiliar or non-intuitive concept to an intuitive and familiar one so that the familiarity and intuitive nature of the latter gets applied to the former. For example, explaining the difference between the national debt and the federal deficit (an unfamiliar and non-intuitive concept) is made significantly more intuitive by making an analogy like so: "federal deficits are like individual trees, and the national debt is like the forest." See how intuitive that becomes because you borrow the intuitive nature of an easy concept, and apply it to a difficult one?

Use simple summary. After describing the non-intuitive, make it intuitive with a simple summary. Just say, "what does it all come down to? [insert what it all comes down to]." For example, I once read an old book written in 1714 about how individual vices ingrained in us by our evolutionary need to compete with each other to pass down our genes are actually highly beneficial at a national, societal, and cultural level because they have broadly beneficial side-effects for humanity as a whole. Clearly, this is non-intuitive. What would a simple summary be? "Private vices are public benefits." Interestingly, that was the title of this famous book that has had a reverberated impact for centuries.

Use description of simple consequences. In business, chances are you're describing a lot of the "how." How will we get this done? How will we avoid struggles along the way? How will this achieve what it is designed to achieve? And that's great and extremely important. But here's the thing: you can make it yet more intuitive with a simple strategy, and that is to describe simple consequences. The "how" is a list of features. But the features have outcomes. And those outcomes are what people use to evaluate a decision. So, explain the how, which is essentially proof, but then say, "ultimately, what will come out of this is [insert simple outcomes]." That provides the simple, intuitive matter needed by the intuitive bias to work in your favor.

Use the "it's simple" refresher phrase. A refresher phrase is a type of transition that frontloads in a sentence a sentiment that is very appealing to human psychology. For example, some refresher phrases are "the big secret is…" "the solution is…" "it's easy…" Why? Because people love secrets, solutions, and ease. Get it? And this "it's simple" refresher phrase frontloads the sentiment of simplicity. It is, in essence, saying, "Listen! This is actually super intuitive, and here's why…" Indeed, this strategy works with all of the methods we are discussing. But also, on its own. When the mind hears one of these, whether it is "it's simple…" or "in simpler terms…" or "essentially…" the intuitive bias is primed. If you then deliver a sentence that fulfills the promise of the refresher phrase, the intuitive bias activates in your favor.

Use alternative balancing. Nothing exists in a vacuum. Everything exists in a complicated ecosystem of alternatives, choices, and opportunity costs. And this is the truth to which our psychologies have evolved over 2,000 years. So, tap into the intuitive nature of choices between alternatives by using the strategy of alternative balancing. What's that? It's simple: saying something along the lines of "we could do [insert option], we could do [insert option], or we could do [insert option]." This is only to be used if you are communicating about what to choose from a set of options, and nobody has intuitively simplified what those options are. For example, when you are figuring out how to respond to a crisis, and after some discussion, the water is still murky, make it less murky (and more intuitive) by saying, "so far, based on what we discussed, it seems like the alternatives are…" Get it?

Use examples. Look, this is simple, and you know what an example is, and how to use one. I'm not going to belabor this. I promised you brevity, didn't I? All you need to know is that examples are incredibly useful tools for activating the intuitive bias. And they are easy, and probably already natural to you. So, use them. Examples (indeed, many of these strategies) do more than just activate the intuitive bias. They activate many components of human psychology in favor of making you appear more credible.

Use cause and effect world-framing. A funny characteristic of human psychology and cognition is how it invents stories out of thin air. Truly, the intuitive bias is *so powerful* that we quite literally build stories out of thin air. And as a part of our ongoing effort to describe the complexity of the world and our lives in simple, straightforward explanations, we always create cause and effect relationships, even if they don't exist. We succumb to the "post hoc ergo propter hoc" fallacy, or in rough English translation, the "after, therefore because" fallacy. In other words, our intuitive bias is so strong that we create cause and effect relationships between things that seem intuitive and likely, but that we have no real evidence to support. Another psychological bias that, in the web of strange tendencies that dominate human cognition, is rather close to the intuitive bias, is the reason bias. What is the reason bias? We tend to deem that things happen for a reason, not randomly; that there is an order to things, and an order ultimately described by cause and effect relationships. So, how do you successfully use cause and effect world-framing? It's simple: just describe non-intuitive explanations through the lens of whatever cause and effect explanations you can find without stretching the truth.

Use conceptualization of simple systems. What does this mean? Well, what is the basic essence of a business system? What is the simplest way to describe a business system? Like this: what goes in and what comes out. The next step in more in-depth system analysis is discussing how what goes in turns into what comes out, but the top-level, simplistic (and therefore intuitive) view is inputs and outputs. And here's the truth: you'll probably notice, if you haven't already, that most business discussions have to do with the how. Think about the role of an executive: executing the functions of the business system. These how-centric discussions are positive, but it is also beneficial to zoom out to the top-level view and simplify the entire system into the inputs and outputs. For example, let's say you are on a team of marketing executives for a big corporation: the second level of system analysis is discussing what actually happens in your proposed system (for example, a proposed marketing plan). The top-level, highly intuitive, and easy-to-grasp description of the system is this: "for every dollar of ad-spend that goes into this system, based on the mechanisms I've described, we will get ten dollars back. One in, ten out." Get it?

Use action-oriented personality descriptions. Human minds are better equipped to successfully and easily interpret descriptions that deal with what things do, rather than what they are. Frames with a relationship of "is" lower ease of interpretation. For example: "Donald Trump is unjust" (X is Y, where Y is a characteristic) is a less intuitive frame than "Donald Trump undermines justice (X verbs Y, where Y is the noun-form of the characteristic). Simply put, one thing *being* another one is less intuitive than one thing *acting on* another. We interpret actions, not equivalencies, with the greatest ease. And we are particularly adept at interpreting actions that imply that the doer or the receiver have archetypal personalities. Archetypal personalities are understandings of personalities in nature that we are born with, or that come extremely easy to us. For example: threat, protector, predator, prey, and victim are all archetypes. Think about it: they are all found in nature. It makes sense that we evolve with an understanding of these personalities. Truthfully, archetypal personalities and evoking them in communication deserve a book of their own. I thought I'd let you in on them now, though. If they seem a little arcane, focus on action-orientation.

Use obvious questions. People are born with the ability to project accurate simulations of the future that an action will create, do so for multiple actions at once, and then choose the best one. What are objective and rational people? Simply people who can perform this counterfactual simulation with greater ease and accuracy. In other words, they give themselves hypothetical paths to choose from that are very realistic. And so, over the long run, they make many good decisions and get ahead. And here's where the intuitive bias comes in: we are so damn good at running these counterfactual simulations (because our ability to survive 2,000 years ago and even today hinges on it) that any information portrayed in the form of a counterfactual simulation is highly intuitive, and activates the bias. So, how do you use this? It's simple. Ask them to imagine a scenario and ask them to consider what they would do if they were in that scenario. For example: "Imagine if you were able to find a marketing system that would yield ten dollars profit for every one dollar spent. You'd jump on that opportunity, wouldn't you? Well, that's exactly what we have in front of us." Or, "Imagine that you were a customer who got offered the package we're pushing in this marketing campaign. You'd go for it, right?"

Use conditional questions. We find conditional reasoning between two variables intuitive. It gets dicey when we get beyond two variables. But with a simple "if X, then Y relationship," we are very well equipped to think with intuitive ease. In fact, how do most of us govern our lives? With perceptual control. What does that mean? We have acceptable limits, and as long as the world is within those limits, we do not act. Only when the world breaks through our limits, are we pushed to action. For example, "as long as this stock as a volatility margin below 10%, we'll hold." It's simple thinking: "if X (volatility margin is below 10%), then Y (we'll hold)." And here's the crazy part: this type of two-variable, perceptual-control-driven thinking is so intuitive that most of us are subconsciously running hundreds, if not thousands, of these loops. It would take too much effort to do it all consciously; one of these loops only jumps into our conscious minds if perceptual control indicates that something breached our acceptable limit. Then, we think about bringing the situation back to homeostasis, within the confines of our limits. So, how do you use this to activate the intuitive bias? Like this: "if X, would you Y?" or "if X, then Y." For example: "if you found a marketing system with this profitability ratio, would you buy it?" Or, "if you want a marketing system with this profitability ratio, this one is for you."

That was a lot.

You got plenty of tools to activate the psychological machinery in your favor.

Just like I promised, right?

But why did I give you so many?

Here's why: the more, the merrier. The more ways you can activate the intuitive bias in your favor, the stronger the positive effects will be. Truthfully, a small handful of these tools working in tandem are more than enough to get it going. But I want you to be a versatile expert.

But there's another reason. And that is that the intuitive bias is particularly important. Why? Because it is the hinge upon which the door of the credibility cascade sits, and has the potential to swing the entire thing. Not to mention that the techniques that trigger the intuitive bias also trigger many similar biases that function in favor of making you appear credible.

But we'll talk about that later.

At the end of the day, think about this: if it cannot be understood, it cannot be seen as credible.

And let me ask you this: who is a true expert? The one who can portray technical mastery of arcane details? Or the one who can make those difficult details intuitive and accessible to non-experts? I would say the latter. And the latter will also be infinitely more credible.

Let's move on.

Incentive-Caused Bias: How to Apply a Secret, Hidden, Little-Known Strategy to Supercharge Your Credibility (You Must Use it Ethically)

By now, you have probably noticed that human psychology works in a host of interesting ways. Perhaps even miraculous ways. And one of the most miraculous functions of human psychology is how effectively our minds can trick us into believing something that we want to believe.

The world is full of con-men.

Tricksters are everywhere.

And many of them use these strategies for evil, not for good.

Yet, here's the sad truth: the biggest con-man out there is none other than our own minds, and we cannot fool anyone easier than we can fool ourselves.

And if credibility is the art of making yourself believed (in honest but sophisticated ways, and for good purposes), and people believe what they want to believe... do you see where I'm going with this?

Here's where I'm going with this: incentive-caused bias.

What is incentive-caused bias?

Simply put, incentive-caused bias is this: people are much more likely to believe something that they want to believe.

So, how do you use this to supercharge your credibility?

It's simple: connect the thing you want people to place faith in, whether it is a plan or a project, to the fulfillment of their goals.

Just any goal, though?

No, not any goal. The most-wanted related goal.

So, in other words: activate the incentive-caused bias by explaining, honestly and subtly, how the thing you are proposing helps the decision-maker achieve their most-highly desired goal that is related to the thing you are proposing (that's why it's called their most-wanted related goal).

Before moving on, let me word the incentive-based bias in this way: people are more likely to believe something they have an incentive to believe. Why do we rationalize bad behavior? For example, why did certain Wallstreet executives rationalize the fraud and deceit that collapsed the economy in 2008? Because the fraud and deceit had a massive incentive attached to it: millions, *billions*, of dollars. When there is an incentive, like billions of dollars, attached to believing something (in this case, the rationalizations for bad behavior), then people are going to believe it. Maybe not all people and all beliefs, but *most* of them, *most* of the time, at least. And that's as close as you can get.

All this talk about incentive-caused bias might make you think it is unethical. Especially if you intentionally activate it to act your favor.

That couldn't be further from the truth.

Like all of these techniques, incentive-caused bias is a double-edged sword.

And the ethical edge is this one: using it to explain the *real* benefits of doing a *good* thing, like the honest financial benefits of implementing an innovative and honest marketing plan.

Get it?

Alright, now that we've got the basics out of the way, one extremely important question remains unanswered.

And that's this: "how do you make people want something?" And now, we get into the long list of scientifically proven tools designed to activate yet another psychological bias in favor of making you appear credible.

I'll promise you this: given the fact that I know of, and have written about, hundreds of methods for making people want something, I'll limit myself to a small handful this time. Indeed, making someone want something is not the lesson of this book; only insofar as it makes you seem credible, are we concerned with making someone want something.

Use interest-alignment. Alignment is a magic word in communication theory. Here it is, as it relates to creating desire in people: if your offer (like a suggested plan, for example) does not directly relate to the interests of the decision-maker, find a way to align it to those interests. How? Find a positive outcome of your suggested plan that ties into what the decision-maker wants. Let me explain. A Venn diagram is two circles that overlap in the middle, in which things are placed in one circle only if they only belong to that category, in the other if they belong only to that category, and in the middle, if they belong to both. All you have to do to achieve successful alignment and activate the incentive-caused bias is to arrange the outcomes of your offer in a Venn diagram where the two categories are "things that this plan does," and "things that the decision-maker wants," and only speak about those items in the middle of the diagram.

Use benefit statements. All people want to do the things they believe will benefit them. It's that simple. The key to getting people to want something is to answer the question, "what's in it for me?" Just pour on the benefits. Pretend someone just asked you the question "what's in it for me?" and you need to apply the fluency and magnitude matrix. Be careful not to oversell; else, it will seem too good to be true.

Use feature-justifiers. In the digital marketing world (in other words, in a world where success depends on making a webpage look credible to visitors), there is an ongoing debate. What gets people to want something? The features of the thing? Or the benefits? Well, it's a false choice: you can have and *should* have both features and benefits. If you had to choose, go benefits. Features alone are not very persuasive. They don't create desire. But benefits alone sound like an oversell. Features are suited to supporting benefits. Think about it: the benefit is the positive outcome; the feature is the aspect of the offer that creates the benefit. In other words: the benefit is the thing they want that your offer does, and the feature is the proof. How do you use this? Well, let me tell you: with a simple speaking pattern. Like this: "[insert benefit] with [insert feature]," or [insert feature] for [insert benefit]," or "[insert benefit] by [insert feature]," or "[insert feature] to [insert benefit]." For example, "This plan achieves 25% higher profitability (benefit) with email list segmentation (feature)." This activates incentive-caused bias, which gives you credibility on its own, in a way that also provides evidence, which is the bedrock of all credibility.

Use benefit tagging. This is a specific type of sneaky benefit-statement that I love using. It's so simple but so powerful. So, you've figured out your decision-maker's most-wanted related goal. What do you do with it? Condense it to a short, simple phrase, and "tag" it onto the ends of your statements. For example, let's say your decision-maker's most-wanted related goal is a better brand image. Benefit tagging would turn "this plan proposes that we appeal to younger demographics to guarantee longevity of demand," to "this plan proposes that we appeal to younger demographics to guarantee longevity of demand, and to build a better brand image." Get it? Just sprinkle that benefit throughout your communication. It works like a charm.

Use the VAKOG senses. What are the VAKOG senses? Visual, auditory, kinesthetic, olfactory, and gustatory. So, here's an example from a previous book of mine that illustrates this perfectly. Non-VAKOG: "You'll be more successful." VAKOG: "You'll see 20% more money when you open your financial statements; you'll hear constant praise from your associates; you'll feel relaxed every day at work; you'll taste the bitter adrenaline of excitement instead of being disengaged." I'll let you decide which one of those is more persuasive (hint: the second one). Note that I left out "olfactory." That's hard to apply to this scenario.

Use loss-minimization. Remember loss-aversion? Avoiding the loss of -$1,000 is, for some, up to twice as desirable as guaranteeing the gain of +$1,000. So, use this principle and do two things to make your offering particularly appealing to your decision-maker: in addition to your positive benefits ("you'll get this"), sprinkle around some loss-avoidance benefits ("you'll avoid losing this"). A common speaking and copywriting pattern amongst effective salespeople is this: "get [insert benefit], without [insert loss or risk of loss]."

Use exclusivity phrases. People want what is scarce. People want what is exclusive. People want the bonus; the limited-supply; the extra. So, how do you activate this natural, psychologically ingrained desire to, in turn, activate incentive-caused bias? By sprinkling exclusivity phrases around your communication. For example, instead of "the portfolio mix produces these results," exclusivity phrases make it "this unique, little-known portfolio mix, fashioned under a non-disclosure-agreement with a special consultancy business, produces these exclusive, unparalleled results with a secret strategy known by no other bank."

Use specific quantification. Individual psychological characteristics pulling people towards the conclusion that you are credible are, alone, powerful. But the force of combined psychological tendencies working in the same direction is a case of one plus one equals three. And specific quantification, in other words attaching a specific quantification to your benefits, activates one other tendency in particular: precision-bias. We'll cover that in its own respect later, but briefly, what is precision-bias? The tendency we have to interpret precise results or promises as more credible. For example, "a $14,943 estimated salary increase" is more credible than "a $15,000 salary increase." It's also known as a crooked number by people who use this strategy to activate precision-bias in online copywriting. 27 is more credible than 30. 4.6 is more credible than 5. 79.3% is more credible than 80%. Get it?

Use problem-solving benefits in a conditional. Remember the medicine concept we covered at the start? And remember the intuitive nature of conditional thinking? This combines those two principles. Make your benefits the solving of a problem that causes pain, otherwise known as a "pain-point," and phrase it in a conditional: "if we want to solve [insert problem], then we should [insert your proposal]." Get it?

Use the benefit-means-justifier structure. What's that? This: "if we want this benefit, these are the means to get it, for these reasons." It's a simple structure that combines a lot of things, namely benefit statements, features, conditional thinking, and evidence. There's not much more to say about this since you know all of its constituent parts.

Use ease statements. There are two types of costs associated with exchanging resources for an offer—money, but also energy in its other forms, like time, or mental calories. And energy is extremely valuable. Think about it: people are often willing to pay more money for convenience. Why? Because energy is a resource; it is valuable, finite, and something people want to conserve. So, what is an ease statement or ease phrase? Any statement designed to minimize the perceived energy cost. Want an example? Here's a generic statement without these little ease indicators sprinkled throughout it: "this process works to get [insert benefit]." And here's the generic statement with an abundance of ease indicators: "this easy, simple, step-by-step process works, and is a straightforward way to instantly get [insert benefit]."

Use minus-inconvenience benefits. Along the lines of ease statements is the principle of not adding indicators of ease but subtracting indicators of inconvenience. For example, let's say there is a common, universally known, stereotypical association between some inconvenience and your offer. Maybe your offer is a new monitoring system for ad performance, and your common inconvenience is a bunch of complicated monitoring spreadsheets. Here's what a minus-inconvenience benefit statement would look like: "and we can monitor our ad performance without getting stuck in the frustrating weeds of an overwhelming spreadsheet." See the inconvenience-words? Like frustrating and overwhelming? See how it's "[benefit] without [inconvenience]?" Simple, right?

Incentive-caused bias is one of the most compelling methods for appearing more credible.

However, it is not a lone-wolf.

Why?

Because, alone, it might seem like selling. Credible people don't sell; they advise from an objective standpoint.

Get it?

They don't persuade, they inform.

A close friend (despite countless dramatic political disagreements) once got me a coaster that said, "I'm not arguing, I'm explaining why I'm right" because she thought that's how I argued. (Probably because of those disagreements, now that I think about it).

Now, despite the humor, the coaster speaks to the truth of credibility: credible people make themselves seen as objective, unemotional, unattached voices of reason who have no stake in the matter; or, rather, who may have a stake, but are not driven by self-gratifying motives.

Relying solely on incentive-caused bias might make it seem like you do have a stake in the matter, which is alright, but that the stake is driving you, which is not.

So, what's the way to protect yourself from this caveat? Simply by not relying on any single strategy alone.

If one strategy were enough, I would write one down, call it a day, and publish the book.

But let me tell you who you have to become: to build a lasting legacy of credibility and start the credibility cascade, you must become someone who understands these strategies so well that they become naturally ingrained in your subconscious mind.

In other words, you must enter a situation knowing exactly which strategies you need to call upon given those unique circumstances, and be able to do so effortlessly.

Now, don't get me wrong. Mere competency is enough for some massive career benefits. But I want to make you an expert, not just merely competent.

If you want that too, stick around. :)

Aesthetic Impact Bias: How to Unlock a Hidden Strategy Creating the Perception of Credibility Without Changing Your Core Message

Now, I've been doing this for a long time.

And by "this" I mean writing books about communication. Whether it is credible communication, or just plain effective communication, or public speaking, I've been at it for a while.

But why am I telling you this?

Here's why: because I want to introduce you to a critical rule that helps me in my study of communication theory and the psychology of influence.

And the rule is called "the JFK rule."

Here it is: if a communication strategy is good enough for JFK, it's good enough for us.

Pretty straightforward, right?

Now, worry not: we'll get into the strategy of activating the aesthetic impact bias, and we'll get into our toolbox for how we activate this bias a well.

But first, let me tell you about a study I first encountered in *Thinking Fast and Slow*, by Daniel Kahneman.

It was fairly complicated, so I'll give you the big picture finding. And it's a finding that revolutionizes our understanding of credible communication.

Here it is: people find language that is aesthetically impactful much more influential and credible than language with the exact same meaning that lacks the aesthetic appeal.

You might be wondering, what does "aesthetic appeal" mean as it relates to language?

And I'll give you an example.

Here's a segment of a particular kind of aesthetic appeal in a sentence I analyzed from one of JFK's speeches (hence the JFK rule). It is a technique called percussive rhythm.

"An example of percussion rhythm is this: "[...] to convert our good words into good deeds [...]" Percussion rhythm is created by several rhetorical components.

Consonance: the recurrence of similar sounds, especially consonants, in close proximity (chiefly as used in prosody – but don't worry about this technique.).

Assonance, a resemblance in the sounds of words / syllables either between their vowels or between their consonants. (While that is the official definition, consonance deals with consonant repetition, and assonance with vowel repetition).

Consonating consonants enveloping assonating vowels.

Starting or ending words with the punchy consonants.

Starting the next word with the last letter in the previous word.

Ending a word with the first letter in the word before it.

Consonance *particularly* of punchy, percussive consonants.

Short, snappy words.

Symmetrical noun forms.

Repetition.

Syllabic symmetry.

Let me prove it if you're skeptical.

Here's what the consonant map of that sentence is: "TTGDDTGDDD." 7 out of 8, or 87.5% of the words in the sentence, had a punchy consonant dominating the phonetics of the word.

Assonance: 7 out of 8, or 87.5% of the words in that sentence, had an "oo" or "o" sound.

Consonating consonants enveloping assonating vowels: in other words, one of the "TGD" consonants that dominate the sentence enveloping the "oo" or "o" vowel sounds. "To convert our good words into good deeds." Check it out: TooToGooDoD - ToGooD. This pattern of assonating "oo" sounds between consonating "TGD" consonants is seen in 6 out of 8, or 75% of the words in this sentence. And one of the two times this pattern (consonating consonants enveloping assonating vowels) breaks is to satisfy another one of the percussion rhythm requirements.

Starting or ending words with the punchy consonants: 7 out of 8, or 87.5% of the words in this phrase start or end with the "TGD" consonants. 4 out of 8, or 50% start *and* end with them (ignoring the pluralic "s" added on to them).

Starting the next word with the last letter in the previous word: "good deeds."

Ending a word with the first letter in the word before it: "to convert."

Consonance, particularly of punchy, percussive consonants: we briefly talked about this, but "TGD" are all punchy and percussive. How do you know? Try saying them. You'll notice a mini "explosion" in your throat. Compare that with non-percussive consonants, like "M," or "N," and how they feel when you say them.

Short, snappy words: 6 out of 8, or 75% of the words in this sentence are one syllable. The average length of the words in this sentence is 4.25. The two words that aren't one syllable are only two syllables.

Symmetrical noun forms (plural): "words [...] deeds."

Repetition: "good [...] good."

Syllabic symmetry: "good [one syllable] words [one syllable] into [two syllables] good [one syllable] deeds [one syllable]." 1 1 2 1 1, with the two syllable word as the line of symmetry.

This sentence is also symmetrical in some other ways: "good (one syllable, four letters) words (one syllable, five letters) into (two syllables, four letters) good (one syllable, four letters) deeds (one syllable, five letters)."

Now, why use percussive rhythm? Here's why: it is captivating, it is memorable, it is attention-grabbing, it is direct, it is clear, it is explosive, and it is distinct."

Let me tell you the secret, though. Throughout the rest of JFK's speech, there were countless phenomenally advanced strategies designed to achieve aesthetic impact. If you thought percussive rhythm was complicated, then you need to know something. Each of the many strategies of compelling aesthetic impact that I will teach you can be nested within each other, over and over; they can ebb and flow; they can phase in and out of each other, to create truly beautiful, captivating language that reverberates through history for decades – centuries, even.

But will it be credible?

Yes. And why? Because it will carry such a gravitas that it will convey complete credibility. And because we percieve the aesthetically pleasing language to be more credible. Not to mention the countless other advantages of this type of language.

So, what are some of these strategies?

Let's get into the techniques you can use to create a powerful aesthetic impact.

Use alliteration: a sequence of consecutive words starting with the same letter (attached alliteration), or not perfectly consecutive, but close together (detached alliteration). For example: "I see also the *d*ull, *d*rilled, *d*ocile, brutish masses of the Hun soldiery plodding on like a swarm of crawling locusts." – Winston Churchill

Use anaphora: starting consecutive phrases, sentences, clauses, or paragraphs with the same words. For example: "We shall not flag or fail. We shall go on to the end. We shall fight in France, we shall fight on the seas and oceans, we shall fight with growing confidence and growing strength in the air, we shall defend our island, whatever the cost may be, we shall fight on the beaches, we shall fight on the landing grounds, we shall fight in the fields and in the streets, we shall fight in the hills. We shall never surrender." – Winston Churchill

Use anadiplosis: using a phrase or word at or near the end of a clause, and then repeating that word or phrase to begin the next clause, or somewhere in the beginning of the next sentence.. For example: "Once you change your philosophy, you change your thought pattern. Once you change your thought pattern, you change your attitude. Once you change your attitude, it changes your behavior pattern and then you go on into some action." – Malcolm X

Use catachresis: using mixed, unusual metaphors that use words and components not commonly associated with one another, but that still create an accurate and intuitive understanding of the subject. For example: "The President's decision yesterday, to set into motion the development of the hydrogen bomb, has placed us on a *knife-edge of history*." – Henry M. Jackson

Use epistrophe: the opposite of anaphora, repeating a phrase or word at the end of a sequence of phrases, sentences, clauses, or paragraphs. For example: "And that government of the *people*, by the *people*, for the *people*, shall not perish from the earth." – Abraham Lincoln

Use personification: assigning human qualities, elements of personality, and intentional action to non-human things. For example: "The tread of time is so ruthless that it tramples even the kings under its feet."

Use sententia: as discussed previously, delivering a summative, punchy, clever, or otherwise compelling sentence that embodies the sentiment of the preceding paragraph. For example: "We are now well into our fifth year since a policy was initiated with the avowed object and confident purpose of putting an end to slavery agitation. However, under the operation of that policy, that agitation has not only not ceased, but has constantly augmented. In my opinion, it will not cease until a crisis shall have been reached and passed. *A house divided against itself cannot stand.*" – Abraham Lincoln

Use anesis: adding a short phrase that minimizes what was just said. For example: "He was one of the most admired men of his time, *yet he had one terrible, fatal flaw.*"

Use appositio: placing together two sets of words, in which the second describes the first (you can also use multiple descriptive phrases in sequence). For example: "<u>John Fitzgerald Kennedy</u>, *a great and good President, the friend of all people of goodwill, a believer in the dignity and equality of all human beings, a fighter for justice, an apostle of peace,* has been snatched from our midst by the bullet of an assassin." – Justice Earl Warren

Use climax: placing the most important, extreme, and powerful item in a list at the end, the least so at the beginning, and the rest in ascending importance from the beginning to the end. Usually accompanied by tricolon. For example: "I think we've reached a point of great decision, not just for our nation, not only for all humanity, but for life upon the earth." – George Wald

Use epitheton: attaching an adjective directly to a noun to enumerate or amplify a quality of the noun. For example: "And on this *fateful* <u>day</u>, with *brave* <u>hearts</u> and *courageous* <u>minds</u>, we march onwards to *uncompromising* <u>victory</u>."

Use expletive: the injection of a short phrase breaking up the flow of the sentence that relates the sentence to the speaker or audience. For example: "The strength of America's response, *please understand*, flows from the principles upon which we stand." – Rudy Giuliani

Use oxymoron: attaching apparently contradictory statements together that, while are literally inherently self-contradictory, speak to a larger figurative meaning. For example: "And *faith* <u>unfaithful</u> kept him *falsely* <u>true</u>." – Alfred Tennyson

Use polysyndeton: intentionally including unnecessary conjunctions in the flow of speech. For example: "You could eat all that you wanted. Many got their first new pair of boots or trousers in basic training after a young life of hand-me-downs. Many will also tell you that before war came to America at Pearl Harbor they were opposed to this country getting involved. But when the Japanese attacked and the Germans declared war they converted overnight and transformed America into a mighty military machine – in uniform *and* factories *and* laboratories *and* shipyards *and* coal mines *and* farm fields *and* shops *and* offices." – Tom Brokaw

Use antimetabole: repeating a phrase in nearly reverse order. For example: "Ask not what your country can do for you, but what you can do for your country." – John F. Kennedy

Use chiasmus: following a clause with another clause that reverses the structure of the first. For example: "His time a moment, and a point his space." – Alexander Pope

Use assonance: the repetition of vowel sounds in consecutive words or in words that are close together. For example: "My h*ea*rt is a h*ou*se h*o*m*ie*, f*ea*r don't live h*e*re." – Curtis "50 Cent" Jackson

Use conduplicatio: the repetition of a key word from one sentence at the beginning of the next. For example: "If this is the first time *duty* has moved him to act against his desires, he is a very weak man indeed. <u>Duty</u> should be cultivated and obeyed in spite of its frequent conflict with selfish wishes."

Use enumeratio: breaking down a noun into a long, descriptive expansion of its constituent parts. For example: "When we <u>allow</u> <u>freedom to ring</u>, *when we let it ring from every village and every hamlet, from every state and every city*, we will be able to speed up that day when all of <u>God's</u> <u>children</u>, *black men, and white men, Jews and Gentiles, Protestants and Catholics,* will be able to join hands and sing in the words of the old Negro spiritual, 'Free at last! Free at last! Thank God Almighty, we are free at last!'" – Martin Luther King Jr.

Use epizeuxis: the immediate repetition of a word or phrase within a sentence. For example: "Isn't it extraordinary that the Prime Minister of our country can't even urge his Party to support his own position?! Yeah. Weak! Weak! Weak!" – Tony Blair

Use paradox: saying two opposite things that seem to be self-contradictory, but are not necessarily so. For example: "I know one thing: that I know nothing." – Socrates

Use rhetorical questions: asking questions with a generally clear, implied answer. For example: "Forty summers have passed since the battle that you fought here. You were young the day you took these cliffs; some of you were hardly more than boys, with the deepest joys of life before you. Yet, you risked everything here. Why? Why did you do it? What impelled you to put aside the instinct for self-preservation and risk your lives to take these cliffs? What inspired all the men of the armies that met here? We look at you, and somehow we know the answer. It was faith and belief; it was loyalty and love." – Ronald Reagan

Use symploce: the combination of anaphora and epistrophe; subsequent sentences, clauses, or paragraphs that start with the same phrase, and end with the same phrase. For example: "When there is talk of hatred, let us stand up and talk against it. When there is talk of violence, let us stand up and talk against it." – Bill Clinton

Use antithesis: contrasting phrases, emphasizing the stark difference between two opposites. For example: "When they go low, we go high." – Michelle Obama

Use asyndeton: the opposite of polysyndeton (adding unnecessary conjunctions), removing grammatically necessary conjunctions. For example: "Duty, honor, *(omitted and)* country: those three hallowed words reverently dictate what you ought to be, what you can be, *(omitted and)* what you will be. They are your rallying points: to build courage when courage seems to fail; to regain faith when there seems to be little cause for faith; *(omitted and)* to create hope when hope becomes forlorn." – General Douglas MacArthur

Use diacope: repeating a word or phrase on either side of an interrupting phrase. For example: "The people <u>everywhere</u> – *not just here in Britain*, <u>everywhere</u> – they kept faith with Princess Diana. They liked her, they loved her, they regarded her as one of the people. She was the people's princess. And that's how she will stay, how she will remain, in our hearts and in our memories, forever." – Tony Blair

Use epanalepsis: repeating the first part of a sentence at the end of that sentence. For example: "*Mankind* must put an end to war – or war will put an end to <u>mankind</u>." – John F. Kennedy

Use hypophora: raising a question and then immediately answering it. For example: "There are those who are asking the devotees of civil rights, *'When will you be satisfied?'* <u>We can never be satisfied as long as the Negro</u>

is the victim of the unspeakable horrors of police brutality." – Martin Luther King Jr.

Use parallelism: consecutive sentences, phrases, clauses, or paragraphs with symmetrical, or "parallel," grammatical structure, and not necessarily similar words in the same positions, but often so. For example: "Let every nation know, whether it wishes us well or ill, that we shall *pay any price, bear any burden, meet any hardship, support any friend, oppose any foe* to assure the survival and the success of liberty." – John F. Kennedy

Use scesis onomaton: repeating a set of words or phrases with essentially identical meaning. For example: "A man faithful in friendship, *prudent in counsels, virtuous in conversation, gentle in communication, learned in all liberal sciences, eloquent in utterance, comely in gesture, an enemy to naughtiness, and a lover of all virtue and godliness.*" – Peacham

Use tricolon: using lists of three. For example: "When President Trump tries to *demean, degrade, and divide*, we have a choice: to give in to doubt and despair, or fight back and show that the power of the people is greater than the people in power." – Cory Booker

Now, I mentioned that you can nest these strategies within one another. The world-moving, earth-shattering speeches of history abound with nested rhetorical devices.

It's truly next-level stuff.

And I love it.

But it's beyond the scope of this book.

(By the way, if you thought those were a lot of strategies, it's nothing compared to the other rhetorical devices that are out there. But going into that would also be beyond the scope of this book).

Anyway, now that you have, at your fingertips, the proven, time-tested, step-by-step rhetorical devices of aesthetic impact, you have exactly what you need to immediately activate the aesthetic impact bias in your favor.

Think about it: why would presidents hire armies of speech-writers to create these beautiful speeches packed full of these strategies?

Here's why: because they understand that the more aesthetically impactful their speech is, the more credibility it will carry.

The tools of presidential speeches are now yours, too.

The Authority-Transfer Principle: How to Instantly Become the Most Authoritative Person in the Room Without Getting a New Degree

You might have been wondering why this book about credible communication hasn't yet touched on evidence.

Well, we're about to.

But this will be much, much more than the standard "use evidence" advice you get from most other places.

On the contrary, I'm going to teach you exactly how to become drastically, dramatically more authoritative by applying a simple strategy to your communication.

It's called the authority-transfer principle.

What is the authority-transfer principle? This: that when you cite a source or provide evidence, you borrow some of the authority the source or evidence carries, which makes you much more credible.

Get it?

The authority of the support you are bringing to the table gets transferred to you.

It's related to the halo effect.

Briefly, what's the halo effect? This: that a positive first impression indicating a positive quality creates an associative cascade around the person that, in turn, suggests a halo of related positive qualities.

So, how does the halo effect relate to the authority-transfer principle? Well, it's simple: when you bring heavyweight evidence to the table in support of your position, that first impression, "this person has evidence," creates a shotgun of related impressions that form a positive halo around you.

What other qualities?

"This person is prepared."

"This person is well-researched."

"This person is informed."

"This person is trustworthy."

"This person is an expert."

"This person is objective."

"This person is thorough."

"This person is devoted."

"This person is *credible*."

The halo effect is why first impressions are so crucial. And here's a warning: it works oppositely too. A bad first impression creates a bad halo. That explains the emphasis on first impressions you'll find in career-counseling services, business books, and the like.

Anyway, back to the authority-transfer principle and how to use it in your favor.

It's simple.

Use evidence: the first step is, obviously, to use supportive evidence, and not just give your word and your word alone as a token of your position. This is where most other books will leave you. Not me.

Use evidence from widely recognized sources: if you're citing someone who nobody knows, that evidence is not going to have much authority to transfer to you. Cite widely recognized sources, and not only *widely* recognized ones, but *positively* recognized.

Use evidence from authoritative sources: if your subject has to do with finance, the Congressional Budget Office is a better source than a small, independent blog.

Use evidence from objective sources: do not, under any circumstances, use evidence from a source that people will recognize as biased towards one particular position.

Use consensus-driven evidence: what's even more powerful than evidence from a widely recognized, authoritative source that is known as objective? Evidence in the form of a wide consensus between widely recognized, objective, and authoritative sources. In other words: "96% of [insert subject] research institutions, including foundations like [insert widely recognized, authoritative and objective example], agree in an overwhelming consensus that [insert claim]." Or, "87% of digital marketing agencies agree that [insert problem], which this program solves, is one of their top three difficulties in this market."

Use quantitative evidence: numbers carry weight, but have a weaker impact than stories. We covered this, and we'll break it down yet more later on, but for now, know this: number-driven quantitative evidence is effective because it gives the logical mind permission to cede to the impact of stories. So, first use quantitative evidence. Simple measurements are easier than pieces of quantitative evidence involving multiple numbers. Why? Every single sentence or segment of a piece of communication has a cognitive load limit. If you exceed it, the understanding of the sentence collapses under the weight of the cognitive load. For example, a simple measurement is "X% of Americans are living paycheck to paycheck." Also, fractional measurements (7/10) are easier to comprehend than percentage estimates, like 73%. Round to a fraction if you can. But what's an example of a piece of evidence involving multiple numbers? "76% of income made in 2019 went to the top 10% of individuals, who own more wealth than the bottom 50% of America." That's tough to comprehend. Maybe not on paper. But remember this: readers can pause, slow down, and reread a sentence; they can control the information-transfer pace. Listeners can't. They have to take in information at whatever pace you are transferring it at; and, if the pace is too fast for them, they check out.

Use qualitative evidence: after appeasing the logical mind with number-driven evidence, use qualitative evidence. A piece of qualitative evidence is, in a way, an example of the quantitative evidence. For example, "7 out of every 10 Americans are living paycheck to paycheck. I once spoke to someone who [insert specific example that is a story of someone who is described by the quantitative evidence]." Quantitative evidence and qualitative evidence are most effective when used in tandem like I showed you. The qualitative is zooming in on a specific example of the quantitative, to express the qualities that are lost in the big-picture numerical analysis. For example, the quantitative paycheck to paycheck evidence misses the qualities of economic desperation, struggle, stress, and loss, which the qualitative examples express. Combining these two types of evidence is yet another case of one plus one equals three. One particularly effective mold is the P Quant Qual P model, which we'll cover later. It is specifically designed to deliver these two types of evidence in a clear, compelling, and credible way.

Use quote-evidence: this type of evidence is simply quoting from a publication or a prime source. Why do this? Because, chances are, that a quote can do something the other kinds of evidence are not so suited for: directly express the stated position of an authoritative person, group of institution. In other words, quote-evidence is directly stating a position that lines up with yours. In fact, we can regard this as a type of qualitative evidence. Take quotes from widely recognized people who are experts in your field. Are you persuading someone to adopt a financial strategy?

Provide a direct quote from Warren Buffet (one of the world's most successful investors) supporting your position.

Use absence-evidence: this one is particularly interesting. It's clever, compelling, and credible. What is absence-evidence? It's saying not what the sources *say*, but what they do *not* say. For example: "virtually no economic research institution endorses the view that [insert policy] is effective at [insert goal]." Or, "virtually no economic research institution has found any major risk of unintended consequences associated with [insert your supported proposal]." Get it? Use both the evidence of addition ("[insert sources] say [insert supporting information]") and the evidence of subtraction ("there is no major [insert type of source – like "economic think-tank"] that says [insert disconfirming piece of information against your stance]").

Use two-sided-preference evidence: who is more credible? The person who reads into both sides of an issue, considers all evidence, takes into account all opinions, and then chooses a side? Or someone who directly jumps to one side of the ideological spectrum? In other words, someone who starts in the middle, and uses evidence to pick a side, or someone who starts on one side, and uses evidence to support that side, ignoring all else? Obviously, the objective observer who starts with no opinion and forms opinions only after considering a wide breadth of evidence is considered more credible. So, how do you create this impression? Well, the first step is to actually do just that: try to understand the other side as best as you can. But the second way is to use two-sided-preference evidence. What's that? It is a speaking pattern that incorporates evidence from one side, and a better piece of evidence from the side you prefer. Get it? For example: "while it is true that [insert opposing piece of evidence], it is also true that [insert supporting piece of evidence], and in this case, [insert supporting piece of evidence] outweighs [insert opposing piece of evidence]." For example, if you are against large executive compensation packages, you can say "while it is true that large executive compensation packages do boost short-term stock value, it is also true that over the long term, profit sharing is proven to produce much higher stock value, and based on the evidence, profit sharing is unequivocally, undeniably, unambiguously more profitable for the firm over time."

Use a plurality of evidence: the more evidence you have, the better. But there's a point of diminishing returns. Bring evidence to the table not only for the sake of bringing evidence to the table, but also for the sake of borrowing its authority until basically anything you say experiences the positive effects of the evidence-based halo effect. Still, the more evidence you have, the better.

Use logical warrants: nearly all argumentative communication can be broken down into three types of statements. First, the claim, second, the evidence, and third, the logical warrants. What are logical warrants? They are the connections between the evidence and the claim. In other words, logical warrants are statements that answer the question, "how does the evidence prove the claim?" And this is a question you must never omit; else, the significance and impact of your evidence will be lost. It's simple: just say, "and the reason this evidence proves that [insert claim] is true is because [insert reasons]."

Use summative sententia: remember the intuitive-bias? Remember how you could use sententia to provide an intuitive anchor for a non-intuitive segment? I recommend that strategy for any situation in which your evidence is complex or non-intuitive. If you are describing a complex study to great depth, once you finish the explanation, just say "what this means is [insert simplest possible form of findings]."

Use visual evidence: we are visual creatures. Any evidence that you can transform into a visual equivalent should be transformed. While we interpret 7 out of 10 easier than we interpret 73%, we also interpret a pie chart indicating the 7 out of 10 split even easier.

Great. You've mastered the art of authority-transfer by way of the right kinds of evidence used in the right ways.

Well done, my friend.

The Values, Beliefs, and Policies Triad: How to Treat Them for Maximum Credibility in Any Communication Situation

The outcome of all communication hinges on the psychology of the mind that receives it, the aggregate mental characteristics of the audience members, and how the speaker's communication interacts with those two things.

And there are three fundamental qualities that you must know how to identify and how to navigate.

Values: the big-picture preferred virtues that people value above all. In America? Some examples are freedom, opportunity, education, capitalism, free speech, equal opportunity, community, sacrifice, democracy, individual rights, constitutionalism, etc. Our most extreme, vicious, and vitriolic arguments are those around values. When someone doesn't share our values, it's almost like we can't truly interact with them in productive, peaceful, ordered ways. We have such drastically different ends in mind that we can never agree on the means.

Beliefs: our general, often unsubstantiated assumptions about the world, how it works, and why things happen. This includes what should happen. Beliefs change in two ways: first, little by little, chipped at over time, or second, in the sweeping after-effects of a tragic or traumatic event.

Policies: statements of "who should do what."

So, how are they related?

Values create beliefs, and beliefs create policies.

The value of freedom creates the belief that a free market is inherently just because it allows for voluntary transactions between free agents, which creates the policy of "Congress should deregulate the financial industry," and probably thousands of others.

Nobody disagrees with values. It's hard to see people arguing against freedom and getting anywhere.

People can disagree with beliefs because while beliefs are derived from values, they can often fork in different directions. For example, two people can be both vehemently in support of freedom (who wouldn't be?), while one believes that a free market is just because it guarantees freedom, and another believes that a command economy is just because free markets can create inequality and inequality can degrade freedom.

Policies are the most wishy-washy.

Policies are what most discussions center around.

Policies are often what you want to present credibly when you are communicating.

See where I'm going with this?

If not, you will.

But first, how do you interact with them?

Never, ever, under any circumstances, at any time, argue against the values of your audience members.

Just don't do it.

You will fail.

I'm warning you.

Values are an incredibly powerful force. So powerful, in fact, that the United States and the Soviet Union brought the world to the brink of total annihilation because of value systems that ran contrary to one another.

They are that important. And if they could get the world's two nations to do that, think about what they can get average people to do.

In other words, think about what they can get people to *believe*; to find *credible*.

So, how do you deal with values? Channel them. When you are advocating for policies or beliefs, and you want to make people believe in them, how do you do it? By channeling the power of values. By making your proposals seem like they both support the values and manifest the values; that they guarantee the longevity of the values and spring forth from the values. "We believe in [insert policy] because we value [insert value]. This policy manifests [insert value] because [insert reasons]. This policy protects [insert value] because [insert reason]. This value is the foundation of [insert policy] because [insert reasons]."

Get it?

The policies that win are those tied to audience values.

Those that don't win are not tied to audience values.

Those that fail miserably go against audience values.

How do people's policies get shot down so easily?

How do strategic competitors poison an idea and kill it on arrival?

How do a small number of simple words create a drastic cognitive impact on an idea's reputation?

Here's how: by convincing others that they undermine one or more critical values.

But what does this have to do with credibility?

Everything.

Credibility is not only the art of getting people to believe *some*thing, but the *right* thing; the starting point of credibility is selecting the right message to present credibly.

And the right thing is the one which channels the tremendous influence of values, rather than going against it.

Get it?

Pay attention to mass communication in the world, whether it is political, commercial, or otherwise.

You'll see, time and time again, these dynamics coming into predictable play.

And now you know not only how to observe them, but how to use them to achieve more credibility.

Wonderful.

The Audience Inertia Principle: How to Use Reverse Psychology and Proven Principles of Audience Attention to Instantly Prove a Point

What if you could instantly (well, not instantly – in about 15 seconds) prove your point with compelling clarity and complete credibility?

You'd want to know how, right?

I'll show you.

But first, let me tell you about this strategy. Let me tell you the psychological forces it brings to the table in your favor.

Social proof: people often go with the crowd, ceding to those around them, and mirroring their actions and beliefs.

This strategy uses social proof.

Visual information interpretation: people easily and intuitively interpret visual information, particularly visual information of other human beings (as in, seeing the way people act). Why? Because in the course of our evolution, seeing and interpreting other people's movements (including micro-movements) and body language conferred an advantage. Why? Well, let's just say that being able to quickly ascertain that "this person will probably try to spear me and steal the berries I gathered" was advantageous back in those dangerous days.

This strategy uses visual information interpretation and the specific kind involving the actions and movements of other people.

Two-way communication: two-way communication (that is, the audience receiving information and then returning information of their own), is significantly more engaging than one-way communication (that is, the audience simply receiving information). Why? Because the act of giving back information draws more of the audience's attention into the immediate situation.

This strategy uses two-way communication.

Memorability: what is memorable will influence us more, over the long run (as we carry it with us and recollect it over and over again), than what is easy to forget.

This strategy is insanely memorable.

So, we must first discuss the different kinds of audiences.

Captive audiences are generally there because they fear some loss if they do not attend; that is, a bad attendance grade if they are students, or the perception of absenteeism if they are employees.

In other words, they are not there because they are thinking, "wow, this speaker is so awesome; I can't wait to be in this meeting because I want to hear what they have to say!"

They are there because they are thinking, "I guess I should go… if I don't, it could hurt my career. I don't want to be seen as unengaged."

Get it?

Voluntary audiences are thrilled to be there solely to hear the speaker speak. Political rallies, for example, are filled with people who are there because they want to hear what the speaker has to say. Or, another example is the self-improvement coach who charges $3,000 per seat at a conference. Those audience members are insanely voluntary; they are so interested in what the speaker has to say that they'll pay a month's rent for it.

Sadly, in the real world, most of our audiences are semi-captive.

But we can use this in our favor.

Like a martial arts expert who uses the momentum of his opponent's strike against him, we can use the major disadvantage of captivate audiences in our favor.

And what's that disadvantage?

That they are unengaged.

And this brings me to the strategy.

It goes like this: ask for a raise of hands in response to a question, with the question phrased in such a way that your point is proven by people *not* raising their hands.

Unengaged people do not hear the question, and when the sudden two-way communication snaps them back to the moment, they won't raise their hands, because they won't know what they're supposed to respond to.

Unengaged people simply don't want to draw attention to themselves by raising their hands.

Unengaged people are *inert*.

And even engaged people are shy, which works against them raising their hands. "I agree with the statement, but what if I'm the only one who raises my hand?" they think, not knowing that everyone else is thinking the same thing.

Want an example? I'll give you one.

Long ago, in college, I gave a speech to try to persuade people into believing, as I did and still do, that the state of the world is good; so good, that it's the best it has ever been.

I wanted to open with a question, asking for a raise of hands, because I knew that two-way communication grabs attention (which is what an opening must do).

But I also wanted to prove two things, which is first, that most people think the world is bad, and second, that they're wrong.

So, instead of phrasing the question as "please raise your hands if you think the state of the world is bad," I phrased it as "please raise your hands if you think the state of the world is good."

In a room of thirty, one hand tentatively shot up.

Just one.

And a *tentative* one.

I knew the audience was captive and mostly unengaged.

I knew they were relatively shy.

I knew that not only were they unengaged, shy, and subjects to audience-inertia, but that most of them actually did not agree that the state of the world is good.

I also knew that if I had phrased it the first way, my point (that people overwhelmingly think the state of the world is bad) would not be proven, because of the audience-inertia principle: my point needed people to raise their hands as proof, and they probably wouldn't have or would have returned inconclusive results.

But because I phrased it the second way, in which the proof was the *lack* of hands in the air, it worked like a charm.

Want some practical examples of this?

Let's say you want to prove that people don't tend to pay much attention to where their products are manufactured, probably in relation to some debate about the overseas-outsourcing of jobs and production.

Your main claim, which you state, is "the truth is that nobody really cares if their clothes are domestically produced, and they probably don't even know where they are made."

To prove it, don't say "by a show of hands, how many of you don't know where your clothes are produced?" Your point is proven by more hands in the air, and because people will likely be inert, you'll get less hands if you phrase it like this. Also, to respond to the poll, people must understand the question rapidly, and "do you not do something, yes or no?" is less intuitive than "do you do something, yes or no?" Think about it: they have a few seconds to evaluate it before they judge it too late to respond.

So, instead, invert it.

Say "by a show of hands, how many of you know where your clothes are produced?" The response will be brilliant: because of audience inertia (and because of the truth that most people do not in fact know), very few people, if any, will raise their hands.

And what have you just done?

Unequivocally proven your point.

Achieved immense credibility.

Portrayed social proof.

Created a memorable situation.

Used visual proof oriented around human action (well, in this case, inaction).

Grabbed attention with two-way communication.

Be careful, though.

I know it's tempting to have your point proven so brilliantly. But make sure this is a wise strategy first.

Because you don't want it to backfire.

So, what do you need to determine before you attempt this?

First, determine that your audience is captivate and relatively unengaged.

Second, determine if shyness will take effect: are there 50 people in the room? Shyness will be a bigger factor in keeping people's hands down. But five? People will be more liberal in drawing attention to themselves.

Third, determine if the audience sentiment is actually aligned in your favor. This strategy won't completely change how people feel; it will emphasize the feelings that are already there, which you want to express, instead of hiding.

Wonderful.

That's a simple strategy for instantly proving any point, before any audience, and grabbing instant credibility for yourself.

And it's quite fun, once you get the hang of it.

In fact, all of these strategies are.

So, not only are you experiencing a tremendous cache of wonderful benefits by using these methods, but having fun in the process.

Irrelevant Damaging Admission: How to Unlock an Easy, Proven Method for Instant Credibility, Trust, and Respect (That is Subtle)

We all do it. We all leave out the embarrassing parts. We all leave out the parts that make us look bad. We all leave out the little details that discredit us. But if you want to achieve massive credibility, stop doing it.

Information is not complete if it is presented in a way that hides your mistakes. Trust me: if you want to be a good communicator, just own up to it. Never omit any details.

Here's the advanced strategy: it's called an irrelevant damaging admission. If your communication omits the details that harm your position, then trust goes down, and the net result is weaker communication.

Let me explain. If you list out 10 positive benefits of your position, your audience will likely perceive a clear bias and adjust their trust coefficient accordingly (from 1 to 0.7, for example), which will yield a trust-adjusted sentiment score of +7 (0.7*10). However, if you make a damaging admission and don't omit, giving 9 positive benefits but 1 harm, your audience sees that you do not omit, and thus they trust you more. The proof of your complete communication and trustworthy nature? You were willing to directly and unequivocally tell them something that undermines your position. So, the net result is a higher trust-adjusted sentiment score: trust remains high, perhaps only decreasing to a coefficient of 0.9. The result? 0.9*9 = +8.1. 8.1 > 7.

Get it? And all you have to do is not omit the damaging details. It will get you respect and trust: as people realize that you prioritize the truth over your image, your image will actually improve. If people realize that you prioritize your image over the truth, then your image suffers.

But here's a key point: it is called an irrelevant damaging admission for a reason, namely that the damaging admission should involve a peripheral, non-core category of evaluation.

If you are describing a plan to lower unemployment, and your damaging admission is that it probably won't lower unemployment, you won't look credible, just silly.

Why? The core category of evaluation is lowering unemployment. That's the one thing your plan can't fail at.

If you are describing a plan to lower unemployment, and your damaging admission is that it might slightly raise the inflation rate while delivering significant bumps to the employment rate, then you will seem credible.

Get it?

The evaluator will think, "oh wow – I have a feeling that these people are hiding the negatives from me, except for this person... they directly told me the truth about a con of their plan. On paper, the others sound better, but I'm not so sure I can believe them. What aren't they telling me?"

This echoes the appeal of moderate candidates in politics, versus more ideologically extreme ones.

I like to sum it up like this: a decent idea fully believed is better than a great idea half-believed.

Your Circle of Competence: How to Avoid the Single Biggest, Credibility-Destroying Mistake People Always Make (Unknowingly)

This is going to seem obvious.

Indeed, it is obvious.

And yet, so many business people make the mistake of ignoring this. Don't take it from me.

Take if from Charlie Munger, billionaire partner to Warren Buffett.

So, what exactly do so many business people forget?

To stay within their circle of competency.

Let me tell you a little about what credibility is *not*.

Credibility is not having an answer to everything.

Credibility is not speaking for the sake of speaking.

Credibility is not jumping out of your area of competency to deliver a credible-sounding stance on something you're – let's face it – **clueless** about.

On the contrary, credibility is knowing what you don't know, knowing what you do know, asking the right questions about what you don't know, and giving the right answers about what you do know.

And it seems easy, right?

It should be. But all too often, professional pressures make it very easy to tread dangerously far outside one's circle of competence.

But trust me on this: the dangers of doing so make it worth bearing the pressures of not doing so.

It's okay to say, "I don't know."

Never speak about something your grasp on is tenuous, because while you won't be saying the words "I don't know," you'll be conveying the words, "I don't know, but I'm trying to look like I do" which is drastically, dramatically more harmful.

Don't know it, but want to provide input for whatever reason? No worries. Know who does know it. Or know how to find it.

But most importantly, know you don't know it, and stay within your circle of competency. And when you're in your circle of competency, be bold and assertive. Why? Because you've earned the right to be.

There's nothing worse than the person who speaks with bold confidence about something they know nothing about.

But there's nothing better than the person who speaks with absolute assertion about something well within their circle of competency.

Think of your circle of competency as your circle of credibility.

Outside of it, there is no credibility to be found; only foolish folly and a degraded reputation.

Inside of it, there is a superabundance of complete credibility waiting for you.

And here's a quick secret: it is said that people who are always learning are the ones who succeed. And what do we know about success? That it demands – indeed, *requires* – credibility.

So, put two and two together, and what we learn is that the people who are always learning succeed because they are always widening their circle of competency, and thus can speak credibly more often, about more subjects.

Amongst Charlie Munger's plentiful gifts to humanity is not only the idea of the circle of competency, but of his iron prescription.

That's what we're going to talk about now.

Charlie Munger's Iron Prescription: How to Always Appear Level-Headed, Objective, and Trustworthy with One Simple Strategy

Ideology drives more people toward making fools of themselves and destroying their credibility than anything else these days.

The consistency bias is our human tendency to maintain intellectual consistency by avoiding the cognitive dissonance (mental discomfort) of holding two conflicting ideas in our mind at the same time.

And the endowment effect compounds the consistency bias. What's that? The added value we place on things we identify with, or see as ours, above their objective, inherent value. What does this have to do with ideology? It applies to beliefs, too.

The consistency bias is the source of many other psychological characteristics, like confirmation bias: the tendency to see new evidence as confirming old conclusions to maintain consistency.

Not to mention the affirmation tendency: that the process of espousing our views makes us believe them yet more. Again, to maintain consistency. It's why debates often do nothing more than solidify the positions of the debaters because, in the process of reaffirming their positions, their belief is strengthened.

And the belief-identification tendency breeds ideology too. We define ourselves by our beliefs, and identity-based cognitive dissonance is one of the most uncomfortable kinds. In other words, holding two conflicting ideas in our mind pains us (cognitive dissonance), but even more so if those conflicting ideas are about who we are (identity-based cognitive dissonance). The psychological benefit of ideology is that it eases the process of shutting out disconfirming evidence, particularly about the beliefs we identify with (which, when disconfirmed, hurt the most).

As we can see, ideology – or a set of irrationally-held extreme beliefs that are strengthened in a snowball-style positive feedback loop – destroys credibility by sowing the seeds of systematic thinking mistakes; mistakes that eventually expose themselves.

The truth will out.

Always.

And the whole point of explaining the consistency bias, endowment effect, confirmation bias, affirmation tendency, and belief-identification tendency was to show you how susceptible we are to slowly, secretly becoming ideologues, little by little, over extended periods of time.

In other words, the chains of ideology are too weak to be felt until they are too strong to be broken.

Why?

Because of the *countless* psychological characteristics that support the formation of ideology, of which I mentioned only the five I find most compelling.

So, if you want to become a credible communicator, and ideology is both easy to succumb to and ruinous to credibility, you probably want to avoid ideology, right?

Enter stage left: Charlie Munger's iron prescription.

It is one of the world's most brilliant pieces of advice on accurate thinking, from one of the world's most brilliant and accurate thinkers.

I came across this prescription for defeating the grim grip of ideology in *Poor Charlie's Almanack* (a book about Mr. Munger), which I happened to be reading when I was writing this book.

I knew I would be doing you a massive disservice if I did not share it in a book about how to become a credible communicator.

So, what's the prescription?

Here it is: in order to avoid the harms of ideology, in order to hedge your thinking against the army of psychological forces that make ideology easy, in order to protect your credibility and retain control of your own mind, you must follow a simple, step-by-step process.

Step one: figure out if you are potentially going to fall victim to ideology, by considering the psychological forces at play in your mind, and how important the subject at hand is to you.

Step two: if there is even a hint *of a hint* of ideology, study the matter until you can argue the position of the opposing side as effectively as they can.

This is the single greatest tool for avoiding ideological thinking, maintaining objectivity, and protecting your credibility.

But, how does this directly tie into credible communication?

Well, not only will you simply *be* a more credible, objective, and intelligent person, but you can also verbalize this entire process.

You can say "while I personally believe [insert position] because [insert reasons], there's another side to this, and they argue that [insert position] because [insert reasons]."

This takes the iron prescription *outside* of you, where others can see it. But at the same time, it allows you to explain your stance. It simply makes your stance more credible.

And that's the whole point, right?

Now, the truth is that this iron prescription is a golden rule of decision making. The scope is not limited to credible communication but extends to the domain of correct thinking.

A very important domain.

Precision Bias: How to Appeal to the First Part of the PUEG Quadrant and Instantly Appear More Credible and Compelling (Simple Strategy)

I'm going to go through this quickly, so follow me here.

When do you need to be credible?

Well, basically all the time, if you want to succeed in business and life.

When do you most frequently need to be credible? That's the better question; the one we can actually answer.

And here's the answer: the most frequent situation that calls upon credibility is when you need a decision-maker to believe that your plan, proposal, or product is the best.

Right?

And the precision bias is perfect for that situation.

So, what's the precision bias?

As I often do, I'll invert the question and tell you what it's not.

It is not that people prefer precise, complex proposals over simple, intuitive ones. They don't. (I tell you this to warn you against misinterpreting the precision bias in such a way that you end up activating psychological forces against you, such as the intuitive bias).

It is not that people find you credible only if you give completely precise measurements supporting your stance. They don't.

It is not that people demand a complex, completely precise train of logic, with all its winding parentheticals, logic gates, conditionals, and mental loops. They don't.

Now, I'll tell you what it actually is: people are biased to prefer the precise solution to their problem, the precise way to achieve something, the precise strategy to get something done.

What do I mean by that? That people find "the exact solution to [insert problem]" more credible than "a solution to [insert problem]."

In other words, people find more credible the precise, specific, exact solution bespoke to their unique problem.

How do you activate the precision bias?

In many ways.

But I want to focus on one that is extremely easy to use.

All you have to do is use one magic word.

Now, while I haven't read the book *Exactly What to Say*, by Phil Jones, I can't help but *notice* it. It is a massive commercial success and is on the subject I write about: effective communication (I say through gritted teeth, quietly plotting to snatch its bestseller spot).

It's funny: the book is essentially about magic words that are inherently influential, and it has the magic word that activates the precision bias in its title.

It's not "what," it's not "say," and it's definitely not "to."

It's "exactly."

This came to me when I was on the phone with a Google Ads specialist, trying to set up some advertisements for a communication course I sell.

He said, "Peter, I know *exactly* what to do for you."

That one word gave him so much credibility in the moment.

He didn't just know what to do for me; he knew *exactly* what to do for me. The solution was a precise fix to my specific problem, like a custom-tailored suit for my abnormally long arms (not joking about the arm thing...)

And think about it: would you rather learn just what to say, or exactly what to say?

The word "exactly" implies a special precision.

Now, I'm sure there are countless words or phrases that do the same thing.

But I can't think of one easier to slip into your communication than this one.

Another way to activate precision bias is to use the audience-identifier enumerator.

This is simply saying who the exact solution is for, where who it is for is exactly who your decision-maker is. For example: "this is exactly how to solve [insert problem] for [insert decision-maker identifier, like small marketing agencies]."

It gets funnier: Phil Jones has a book called *Exactly What to Say for Real Estate Agents.*

I'll let you fill in the blanks.

Now, the precision bias is just one of the biases in my poorly named PUEG quadrant.

What's the PUEG quadrant?

I'll reveal the "U" now.

Uniqueness Bias: How to Appeal to the Second Part of the PUEG Quadrant, Easily Earn Trust and Quickly Grab Undivided Attention

So, precision is the exact solution for the exact type of decision-maker you are trying to present credibility to.

What's uniqueness?

Well, it's another bias, just like the precision bias.

And it makes one thing appear much more credible than another to someone who has to decide between them.

So, what is it not?

The uniqueness bias is not that people find eccentric, unusual proposals more credible than standard ones. They don't.

The uniqueness bias is not that people will believe the person with a unique set of credentials. They don't.

The uniqueness bias is not that people will gravitate to that which stands out. They don't.

What is it, then?

The uniqueness bias is that the *singularity* is most compelling.

In other words, "this is the action that will solve [insert problem]" is less compelling than "this is the single action that will solve [insert problem]."

People have a mental model of problems as locks and solutions as keys.

And there's usually a single key to each lock.

People would rather do one single thing to solve a problem. One simple, intuitive fix appears more credible than a solution that is really just a package of many solutions.

That's the uniqueness bias.

Just like you activate the precision bias with the magic word "exactly," you activate the uniqueness bias with the magic word "single."

I also like to call this the "self-contained bias."

Why do we find the unique, single solution more credible than the complex package of solutions?

One of the many reasons is that we counterfactually simulate impacts of the solutions long into the future.

The package of solutions is interdependent. A complex proposal with many moving parts must have all of the moving parts working as they were designed to work. There's much room for failure.

The single solution is stand-alone and self-contained; it is dependent only on itself. It is one unit. It interacts with the system it is fixing, not a handful of other units trying to fix the system at the same time.

In short, people find "the single solution" more credible and tempting than "one of many solutions," or "a handful of solutions stitched together."

People will rather do one single action to solve a problem, rather than manage the complicated implementation of a web of interdependently linked solutions that fall apart if there is one weak link in their ranks.

And

Simplicity Bias: How to Appeal to the Third Part of the "PUEG" Quadrant to Achieve Yet More Credibility with a Simple Set of Words

So, we've got precision: people want the exact solution.

And we've got uniqueness / self-containment: people want the single solution more than the multi-faceted host of solutions.

So now, we turn to the ease bias, also known as the simplicity bias.

Remember the intuitive bias? People find straightforward, intuitive arguments more credible then complicated lines of convoluted logic.

Remember the incentive-caused bias? People believe – or find credible – that which they have an incentive to believe. And remember how we activate it by presenting our solution as an easy solution?

Well, the simplicity bias evokes both the intuitive bias, the incentive-caused bias, and the ease-preference bias (also known as laziness).

People find the simplest solution the most credible.

People believe that the least complex solution is the most reliable.

People hate wasting mental calories, and thus have an incentive to avoid complexity; this incentive causes them to question complex solutions with lots of moving parts, simply because they use up mental calories and seem, because of their complexity, to have a lot of ways they can break.

What does this all come down to?

This: the fact that a simple solution is more credible than a complex solution.

The same forces empowering the uniqueness bias are at play in the simplicity bias.

So, for the precision bias, your magic word is "exactly."

For the uniqueness bias? "Single."

What about the simplicity bias? Well, it's a simple word. The word? "Simple."

You'll see how we will activate all of these biases in tandem, working in the same direction (in your favor), with a simple, step-by-step formula.

Why are we doing that, though? Because a host of biases pushing people to the same conclusion is drastically more effective than each of the individual biases on their own. And the biases can conflict: they can operate in opposite directions. They can cancel each other out.

In other words, we are going to discover a formula to activate the precision bias, the uniqueness bias, the simplicity (also called ease) bias, and the guarantee bias (which is up next), for two reasons: first, because they are more powerful in tandem, and second, because this makes sure that they are all on your team, and not infighting amongst themselves like petty siblings.

So, that's the simplicity bias.

It's pretty simple, right?

Guarantee Bias: How to Appeal to the Fourth Part of the "PUEG" Quadrant with a Proven Strategy to Immediately Create Credibility

Alright, this is the fourth and final part of the "PUEG" quadrant. But we'll get into that later.

First, let's talk about the guarantee bias.

Here's the truth: there's a trope out there that mocks guarantees in persuasive communication.

Think about it: the door-to-door salesmen trying to meet his quota with slicked-back hair knocks on the door, gives his frantic pitch and says the word "guarantee" in oxymoronic superabundance.

It's in countless movies, shows, books, and articles.

So, we discount it, without realizing how important it actually is.

First, let me explain a hidden component of human psychology.

When we are evaluating decisions with monetary value, for example, we are willing to pay a mathematically irrational amount of money for the reduction of risk. For example, let's say you are purchasing 100 financial securities, with an estimated payout of $100 per each security, in one year. Let's say the average risk of failure is 10%. So, on the net, there is a high chance that 10 out of the 100 securities will fail, yielding nothing.

That's offer number one.

Offer number two is 100 financial securities with an $80 payout per each security in one year, with a 0% failure rate. In other words, it's guaranteed that none of the securities will fail.

Which offer is better?

Rational financial theory dictates that we calculate the EMV, or expected monetary value, by performing this operation: 100*$100*90%

(number of securities in offer one multiplied with the expected payout per security multiplied with the fraction of the securities that are expected to follow-through). This yields an expected monetary value of $9,000 for offer one.

What about offer two? 100*$80*100% yields an EMV of $8,000.

So, rationally, 100% of people with basic arithmetic skills should select the first offer, especially because larger sample sizes (like 100) regress to a mean more reliably than smaller sample sizes, which produce abnormal results.

But people are not rational.

Studies show that in situations mirroring this dynamic, people will overwhelmingly select the no-risk option, and potentially cost themselves $1,000 in the process.

That's called risk-reduction hyper-response tendency.

It's also called risk-aversion.

In fact, it is called many things by many different people because this discipline is still in its early phase of development.

But, whatever you want to call it, it comes down to one thing.

We emotionally overweigh the value of risk-proofing a package.

When the numbers are this clear, it's not as likely that the risk-reduction hyper-response tendency will come into play as it does in messier, muddier real-life scenarios. Why? Because in this case, it costs less mental calories to reason out the respective value of each package, and there is less emotion staked on a hypothetical analysis.

Why does risk-reduction hyper-response tendency happen? Probably because of loss aversion. If you forgot, that's how we feel a loss more than an equivalent gain. In other words, losses hurt us more than gains pleasure us, and for some people, twice as much.

It all comes down to this: people will exchange an illogically high amount of resources for the reduction of a small risk to no risk.

So, now we'll get into the guarantee-bias.

People find guarantee-associated solutions more credible than non-guarantee-associated solutions.

But how do we activate it?

Think about the precision bias, uniqueness / self-containment bias, and the simplicity / ease bias.

How do we activate those?

By sprinkling some magic words into our communication.

This is no different.

And what's the magic word? "Proven" is my favorite word that activates the guarantee-bias.

What does it all come down to? That "this solution" is less credible than "this proven solution," and that a solution with no associated guarantee is less credible than one with a compelling guarantee.

But you might be thinking, "what if I can't guarantee anything?"

Guarantees are always possible.

Guarantees are not necessarily that the solution will produce some set of results. These guarantees are foolish and have a reputation for being the tool of fishy salesmen.

There are no guarantees in life.

The one who guarantees something outside their control is not credible.

This is a topic of debate. But I say, never guarantee external results. That's my advice. And it's based on the simple truth of the fact that guaranteeing something you have no *real* control over is a proven way to undermine your credibility.

But that doesn't mean you can't give result-associated guarantees.

The golden rule is this: that you guarantee something actually in your control.

For example, don't say, "I guarantee that you will get at least a 20% boost in your return on investment." That's guaranteeing something you don't control. Instead, say, "I guarantee that if we do not make you at least a 20% return on your investment, we will give you a no-haggle, full refund and instantly refer you to a competitor better equipped to handle your business than we are. And I'm not just saying this. Check page three of the contract. There's nothing to lose here."

See what I mean?

Which is more powerful?

No, really... which is better? A beautiful, outstanding proposition half-believed or a great proposition fully believed?

So, to further tease out our golden rule of guarantees, here it is: don't undermine yourself and be dishonest by guaranteeing something that's outside of your control. Instead, guarantee what's in your control and follow through.

And there are many more ways to correctly guarantee something (and therefore improve your credibility) than the one I showed you.

Use performance-guarantees. "I guarantee that we will hire yet more new employees who will be fully devoted to this account and beating your performance expectations." Note that you are not guaranteeing that you will beat those expectations, but that you are fully devoted to it, and will hire people to satisfy it.

Use methodology-guarantees. "I guarantee that we will only use EPA approved, sustainable production methods to ensure that you are helping, not hurting the environment."

Use superior-approach guarantees. "I guarantee that we will be using the best-known approaches to supercharging your digital marketing channels and that we will always be learning the new methods as they are created by platform innovation."

Use superior-knowledge guarantees. "I guarantee that the collective experience we will have servicing your account will represent the best knowledge in this field."

Use accessibility guarantees. "I guarantee that we will pick up your phone call without a moment of placing you on hold."

You can guarantee many things, without guaranteeing the incredible. If you want to be credible, don't promise the incredible.

Why be conservative with guarantees? Because reputation matters. Remember the ad-hominem fallacy? Think about it: once you break an incorrect-guarantee (a foolishly made promise of externals you can't actually control), all of your future guarantees lose their impact, your reputation is tainted, and your credibility can be irreparably damaged.

I will repeat it: never guarantee something outside your locus of control. If it doesn't undermine your credibility from the start, it will if the guarantee falls-through.

But that's just my two cents.

Alright.

We've done precision, uniqueness / self-containment, simplicity / ease, and now guarantee.

Let's see how they come together for maximum impact and massive credibility.

I warn you: this is a fair bit complicated.

You might want to read it twice over. It's worth the time.

The 4x3 Formula: How to Use a Quadruple Tricolon to Satisfy the "PUEG" Quadrant (In One Simple, Step-by-Step Formula)

When we were discussing each of the biases and their activating words, I gave you one main magic word for each one.

You can activate the precision bias with the word "exactly."

You can activate the uniqueness / self-containment bias with the word "single."

You can activate the simplicity / ease bias with the word "simple."

You can activate the guarantee bias with the word "proven."

And here's the kicker: you can activate all four biases in the same direction in one sentence with these four words.

And if you want yet more impact? You can activate each bias by using a tricolon phrase devoted to each bias and stacking four of these sentences together.

But how? If a tricolon phrase uses comma-separated lists of three, and there is one magic activator-word for each bias, how can you make a tricolon for each bias?

Well, let me tell you.

The truth is that there isn't just one word per bias.

I'm sure you've figured that out.

The precision bias is also activated by words like "precisely," "specifically," and "tailor-made."

The uniqueness / self-containment bias is also activated by words like "only," "individual," and "one."

The simplicity / ease bias is also activated by words like "step-by-step," "straightforward," and "easy."

The guarantee bias is also activated by words like "time-tested," "evidenced," and "confirmed."

And these words have near-synonymous meanings to the four magic words. But stacking them together heightens their psychological impact. Remember the rhetorical device of scesis onomaton? Repeating phrases with nearly identical meaning?

For example, "a man faithful in friendship, prudent in counsels, virtuous in conversation…"

Each of the tricolon items means virtually the same thing.

But here's the secret: even the ancient masters of rhetoric, like Aristotle, understood the strategy of "micro-repetition."

What's that?

The more times someone hears a message, the more they are likely to believe it. This is a psychologically proven fact of human intuition. Without realizing it, the more we hear a message, the more we believe it. This is the power of positive affirmations, for example. The more you say to yourself, I don't know... maybe, "I'm going to be a phenomenal public speaker," the more you will believe it, and the more you believe it, the more likely it is to come true.

So, we've established that repetition is an incredibly powerful tool of persuasion, right? Well, not quite. Why not? Here's an example: let's say you want to persuade your audience into believing that your proposed solution is the single solution that can solve their problem. You can't quite say the following: "This solution is the one solution that can solve your problem. This solution is the one solution that can solve your problem. This solution is the one solution that can solve your problem." Thus, we arrive at the inevitable, indelible limitation of the power of repetition. Speaking that way has the opposite effect, and will drive people away. I want you to keep this in mind, too: in this example, we repeated the message three times in 33 words.

But guess what? We can easily overcome that limitation, unlock the persuasive power of repetition, avoid seeming crazy, and actually make repetition more persuasive. How? Micro-repetition. So, instead of repeating it three times, making the point three times in 33 words, and seeming a little crazy and off-putting, we can say this: "This *unique, specific* solution is the *one, single, individual* key that *alone* can solve your solution *in an unmatched way.*"

Get the unbelievable power of what I just showed you? You repeated the sentiment (that it is the one solution) 7 times in 20 words. That's a major improvement. Thus, micro-repetition is the solution to the limitation of persuasive repetition.

Get it? Moving on now, to the 4x3 formula.

It uses the precision bias.

It uses the uniqueness / self-containment bias.

It uses the simplicity / ease bias.

It uses the guarantee bias.

And it uses the power of micro-repetition with tricolons built around the device of scesis onomaton.

To rephrase that, it uses repetition of synonymous single words (micro-repetition) in lists of three (tricolon) that mean roughly the same thing (scesis onomaton).

Sounds complicated? It won't be once I show you an example.

Here it is: "This specific (1), tailor-made (2), precise (3) solution (scesis-onomaton oriented tricolon satisfying the precision bias) caters *exactly* to solving [insert problem] for [insert audience identifier] by [insert method]. It is the one (1), single (2), individual (3) action (scesis-onomaton oriented tricolon satisfying the uniqueness / self-containment bias) that can *alone* solve [insert problem] without [insert associated inconvenience]. And, for your benefit, it is broken down to a simple (1), straightforward (2), step-by-step (3) process (scesis-onomaton oriented tricolon satisfying the simplicity / ease bias) that won't waste your time and energy, but quickly give you [insert benefit one], [insert benefit two], and [insert benefit three]. We also want to say that if you adopt this proven (1), time-tested (2), confirmed (3) strategy (scesis-onomaton oriented tricolon satisfying the guarantee bias) for solving [insert problem] and getting [insert benefits], we guarantee [insert results] or your money back."

Why do I call it the 4x3 formula? Because, it is four sentences, each devoted to one of the four PUEG biases, that use tricolons to achieve micro-repetition of bias-activating words. It also uses associated strategies we went over, like a correctly-made guarantee, non-tricolon micro-repetition of other bias-activating words, and audience identifiers.

Doesn't seem so complicated now that we've gone over it, right?

Before we move on, I want to introduce you to one final strategy.

The strategy? *Squishing.*

In other words, you can scrunch down the 4x3 formula into one sentence, like you can collapse an accordion. It will retain its credibility-boosting properties, just on a proportionally smaller scale.

For example: "this one (uniqueness bias activated) simple (simplicity bias activated), proven (guarantee bias activated) strategy is the exact (precision bias activated) solution to [insert problem]."

Get it?

Now, let's quickly talk about spectrums. Remember spectrums? That your audience suffers from mental malleability; in other words, that your communication inputs change their mental states in ways that can work both for and against you, as the communicator, and that mental states can be described as one to ten spectrums for a set of qualities?

Well, perception of precision, perception of uniqueness, perception of simplicity, and perception of guarantee are four important spectrums.

And here's the caveat: I refuse to promise that these strategies, whether it's the sprinkling of magic words or the full-on 4x3 formula, will instantly move your listeners from a one to a ten on these spectrums. I simply promise that, *ceteris paribus*, the effect of these strategies will be edging them up on those spectrums, and that, *ceteris paribus*, those spectrums will activate psychological biases that will make you appear drastically more credible, which, *ceteris paribus*, will make you dramatically more successful in life.

When it comes to credible communication, there is no silver bullet.

There are thousands of external variables.

And I will not mislead you about that.

Others will conveniently forget to tell you that while these credibility-producing strategies do make you more credible, that credibility-boost won't necessarily outweigh things that might be working in the opposite direction.

He who does not pay heed to the inherent complexity of life when advising others does them a disservice.

Alright. Let's move on from the PUEG business.

Kairos: How to Apply the Single Most Important Credibility-Enhancing Concept to Real-World Communication Scenarios (With Ease)

Let's say that you can choose one of two scenarios in which to deliver your speech. Assume that everything about the speech is the same.

Same words.

Same delivery.

Same everything.

The only difference is *when* you give the speech. And the goal is to persuade a company to change its operations.

Here's scenario one: everything is absolutely wonderful. Profits are high, management is handing out chunky bonuses, and everyone is getting a raise.

Here's scenario two: everything is absolutely awful. Profits have tanked, management is taking bonuses *back*, and there are no raises to speak of.

In which of those scenarios would a speech to persuade a company to change its operations actually succeed?

When it is abundantly clear that the operations aren't working.

Why?

Because you do not speak in a bubble. The facts of the outside world always influence your audience. Again, context is everything.

Will people want to change the way a company works when everything is wonderful? No.

How about when everything is awful? Most likely.

Kairos is incredibly powerful. You are making the outside world your partner in persuasion. You are using an amazing persuasive element: the reality of the lives your audience members are living.

In other words: they will never ask, "what's the evidence?" if they are living the evidence. We see Kairos being used by politicians all the time, and they probably don't even know it.

Every time a politician speaks of economic reform during a stock market crash, that's Kairos.

Every time a politician speaks of adding a traffic cop after a massive jam, that's Kairos.

Every time a politician speaks of making Mexico pay for a wa... you know what? Let's not go there.

But you get the point.

Timing is everything. Save your persuasion for when it is most likely to succeed. You will add the most powerful persuasive element to your speech, without even changing the words.

Correctly timing your communication – which is all Kairos is – is one of the biggest possible boosters to credibility.

I promised brevity, but Kairos is so important that I want to explain it in as many ways as possible. I want to make sure that your understanding of Kairos is so fluent and innate that you never miss an opportunity to employ it in your favor.

So, to that end, here's how I described Kairos in my first book, *How to Master Public Speaking*: "This is the dictionary entrance for Kairos: 'Kairos (καιρός) is an Ancient Greek word meaning the right, critical, or opportune moment. The ancient Greeks had two words for time: chronos (χρόνος) and kairos. The former refers to chronological or sequential time, while the latter signifies a proper or opportune time for action. While chronos is quantitative, kairos has a qualitative, permanent nature. *Kairos* also means *weather* in Modern Greek. The plural, καιροί (*kairoi* (Ancient and Modern Greek)) means *the times*.'

The concept of Kairos is, perhaps, much more fundamental than even ethos, pathos, and logos. It simply means biding your time. It means waiting to attempt persuading people until a time comes when persuasion is most likely to work.

In business, for example, if you have a radical new way of doing things that challenges the status quo of company operations, then Kairos is your friend. Unless you are sure of your ability to persuade the organization to adopt the change you want to see, then simply bide your time. Wait, and while you wait, keep developing your idea as well as a plan for implementing it. Keep it at the ready, but keep it concealed.

Eventually, there will be a time of crisis. Investors will get cold feet, manufacturing will fail, a public relations scandal will occur, etc. As Kairos suggests, the time of crisis will be the time to attempt to persuade the company to change its operations. That is because, during this time of crisis, people are especially persuadable and willing to try new things. The status quo is not working, and thus they will be much more malleable and open to your ideas.

Wait for the opportune time, and use your persuasion when it will be most effective. If you can combine ethos, pathos, logos, reciprocity, authority, scarcity, likeability, consensus, and consistency with kairos, then you maximize your persuasive power. Don't give a speech trying to persuade a company to change the way of doing things when the status quo is working and people are happy. Wait for the status quo to fail, and once it does, your persuasive power will be maximized. A huge part of using Kairos to your advantage is tuning in to the motions of collective opinion. Any group tends to experience opinion-convergence: over time, given no drastic changes, many common opinions will develop within the group. Be sensitive to these collective opinions, especially when they might be in flux. That will help you find the right time, and as you may have heard, timing is everything."

Concessions: How to Use a Reverse-Psychology-Based Secret to Boost Your Credibility Whenever There is Disagreement in the Room (Often)

It takes a brave and honest person to admit that an opponent is correct about something. To concede that an opposing idea to yours is indeed partially correct is an action most speakers would never imagine themselves doing. Why would you ever want to admit that an opponent might actually be correct about something? Particularly if you are speaking to inform or persuade, a crucial feeling your audience has to have towards you is trust.

In the case of an informational speech, your audience must trust that you know what you are talking about and that you are impartial. In the case of a persuasive speech, your audience must trust that you aren't holding anything back from them in order to make another sale. To make a small acknowledgment of an opposing viewpoint is to build trust in you. Why? Because it shows that you are impartial and that you are not holding anything back. Trust is one of the most important elements of a successful speaker to audience connection.

For a successful concession, make sure to keep it brief. You don't want to spend too much time talking about an opposing viewpoint. That's not the aim of a concession. What you say about the opposing viewpoint isn't important as long as it's an acknowledgment of partial validity.

For a successful concession, try to use a format like this one: "Supporters of [product, person, or idea] often say [the opposing benefit]. I actually agree with them that [insert benefit] is important, but I would argue that [your product, person, or idea] accomplishes [the opposing benefit] even more, for [reasons and evidence]. And unlike [product, person or idea], [your product, person, or idea] has [additional benefit(s)]." As you can see, this format allows you to acknowledge an opposing viewpoint, which builds trust, and then use that to transition to talking about your viewpoint. You do not agree with your opponents that their idea is better. You agree with your opponents that a certain benefit is important, and then show the audience that your idea actually has more of that benefit.

High-Ground: How to Appeal to the Undeniable Truths, Appear Wiser, and Achieve Credible Communication with One Simple Strategy

In arguments, even those in professional settings, adults can act like children. And the high-ground strategy guarantees that you will be the remaining, reigning adult in the room.

So, let's get into the background.

Remember the ad hominem logical fallacy? It is arguing "against the person" instead of against their statements. Remember how we are so innately drawn to this logical leap that it is a cognitive bias that you can use in your favor?

Well, one of the most common forms of the ad hominem fallacy is the closely related hypocrisy fallacy.

What's that? It is the tendency to argue against the person by pointing out the hypocrisy in their argument.

And there are three types of hypocrisy.

Organizational hypocrisy is when someone says, "your organization does it too!"

Individual hypocrisy is when someone says, "you do it too!"

Argument hypocrisy is when someone says, "you once said X, which is inconsistent with what you are saying now!"

But doesn't it just seem natural that people should practice what they preach? It does; our gut instinct tells us that yes, people should themselves do that which they prescribe for others. But logically, a hypocrite is not inherently wrong.

If I say "don't spend all your money in a slot machine," and then spend all my money in a slot machine, is my original advice suddenly incorrect because I went against it? Obviously not.

Sadly, I see the ad hominem and the hypocrisy fallacy play out in debates everywhere. And not just any debates, but those at the highest levels, between extremely intelligent and sophisticated people, even those running for the highest office of the land.

And I have a feeling that they know the illogic of the ad hominem and hypocrisy fallacy approach, but that they also know just how compelling these types of arguments are; just how intuitive they are to the people listening.

Think about it: our brains want to conserve mental calories, so they take shortcuts. One of the shortcuts is, instead of evaluating the difficult question of "what do I think of this message?" substituting the easier question of "what do I think of the message's source?" We do this constantly, and oftentimes, this mental shortcut is correct. But we cannot rely on it when we want our logic to drive us.

And not only are mental shortcuts like this one often correct, but they are necessary. We simply do not have the mental resources to go without them. Think about living life without defaulting to habit structures; imagine having to make every single decision, no matter how small, all over again, every single day. It would be madness. These shortcuts serve a valuable purpose. But we must push ourselves beyond them to achieve logical clarity and, thus, compelling credibility.

Most of these other credibility-boosting strategies involve channeling a mental shortcut, a feature of psychology, or an element of human cognition such as a bias in your favor.

Not this one.

This one is gaining credibility not by flowing with the biases and using them in your favor, but plainly going against them. Not in the minds of your audience members, but within yourself.

You'll see what I mean.

So, now that we have the background down, let's get into this strategy: what it is, and how to execute it.

The high-ground approach is leaping out of the weeds and muck of ad-hominem and hypocrisy-driven disagreement, and appealing to an elevated, mutually agreeable position which nobody would dare disagree with.

For example, in a heated debate and negotiation about a merger between two firms, one might hear something like this: "your firm has practiced aggressive accounting that is so dishonest it would make someone ashamed of the entire human race. Since we are carrying liability from this, we deserve to maintain more of our personnel than you."

The temptation is to say, "that's actually not at all true, you liar, and your firm has actually performed more aggressive accounting than anyone else in the industry. We're keeping our people."

So, what do we have here? Two people who accused each other of dishonest accounting, who are likely not going to reach an agreement, who bruised each other's ego, and who are going to leave empty-handed.

Do you think the tempting response, the hypocrisy-based ad hominem, is credible? Do you think it is persuasive or influential? Do you think it builds consensus and drives results?

Once again, I find myself saying "obviously not."

So, what's the response that stems from this high-ground strategy?

Something like this: "look, while we push our accounting a little, we have not been drastically more aggressive than anyone else in the industry, and there won't be any liability involved for you. In fact, I have just sent our documents to your accounting department for verification. But that's not the point, because this isn't about the past, but about guaranteeing the best possible future for our joint endeavor; and to that end, I think we should tackle all questions of personnel on the merit of the people involved, and their ability to contribute to the future we want."

Do you see how it says "X doesn't matter, Y does" where X is the source of the ad-hominem, and Y is a mutually agreeable elevated stance that is salient to the desired outcome? In this case, X is the alleged aggressive accounting from one firm, and the elevated stance Y is guaranteeing the best possible future for the merging firms.

It's not getting angry or aggressive.

It's not responding to the attack with a counterattack.

It's not vehemently denying the charge. Your calm will do that for you, in addition to a direct but short statement like "we have not been drastically more aggressive than anyone else in the industry, and there won't be any liability for you," coupled with decisive, action-driven proof, like "in fact, I have just sent our documents to your accounting department for verification."

Get it?

The power of this strategy comes from the contrast between the petty source of the ad hominem attack, and the gravitas of the elevated stance.

The power of this strategy comes from breaking the expectation that an attack will be followed by a counterattack

The power of this strategy comes from boosting your credibility by leaping out of petty disagreement into the domain of an undeniable statement, appealing to superior values.

Values strike again.

The Justifier Strategy: How to Avoid the Biggest Credibility-Destroying Mistake and Activate the Reason-Gate Bias for Fast Compliance

This one is particularly fascinating. (Actually, the truth is that they all seem that way when I am writing about them. The one I'm currently writing always seems to be the most interesting one to me – a cognitive bias I'm performing, called the availability / recency bias. This one does not make its way into this book).

So, what is the justifier strategy?

Well, it's simple.

Let me paraphrase an often-repeated study into the nature of human compliance, and what can get more of it.

People in an office are waiting in a long line for a printer.

The experimenter cuts the person in front, in one of three ways.

One way is for no reason, with no justification. Just "can I cut you?" This has very low compliance from the person.

Another way is with a justifying reason. "Can I cut you because I need to be in a big presentation in five minutes?" This has the highest compliance from the person.

The last way is with a reason, but one that doesn't actually justify the request. "Can I cut you because I need to print these documents?" Here's the kicker: this only had *moderately* less compliance than the reason that actually justifies the request.

The conclusion? People respect reasons; they demand that actions are justified by a reason, and often simply need to hear a reason without identifying if it logically supports the action.

In other words, human minds have a checkbox corresponding to something like this: "does this have a reason for it?"

And the truth of the reason, and whether or not it justifies the action, takes a backseat.

And this checkbox must be satisfied before you achieve credibility and the compliance that comes with it.

So, no reason is the worst.

Any reason is much, much better.

A reason that actually makes sense is only moderately better than any reason.

It all comes down to this: we often look at reasons and judge not their quality, but their existence.

My advice is not to use fake reasons. I only explain this so that you understand the importance of reasons. The fact that any reason is significantly more credible than no reason is not an argument for producing fewer real justifiers, but more… lots more.

And here's what it comes down to. To appear more credible, you must justify every claim you make with an abundance of logically-sound reasons.

But there are two kinds of justifiers.

Justifiers and meta-justifiers.

Justifiers are "[insert claim] because [insert reasons]."

Meta-justifiers justify why the communication itself is actually happening.

"I want to tell you this because [insert reasons]."

"The reason we should talk about this is [insert reason]."

"I am calling to [insert reason]."

The meta-justifier reasons can be the source of a lot of rhetorical strength that grabs attention quickly and easily.

Why?

Because you can strategically design the reasons to be more compelling to your audience members.

How?

Use benefit-driven reasons. For example, "I want to tell you this because this information can reduce your expenses by 30%, simplify your production process, and reduce the risk of a bottleneck, so you make more money with less effort."

Use urgency-driven reasons. For example, "I want to tell you this because soon it will be too late to act on this information, and I want to make sure you don't miss the chance."

Use loss-aversion-driven reasons. For example, "I want to tell you this because without this information, you are significantly more likely to suffer from inefficient production processes, a major leak of wasted resources, and weaker market capitalization."

Use scarcity-driven reasons. For example, "I want to tell you this because nobody else knows it as of now, and you can use it to get a first-mover advantage."

Use opportunity-driven reasons. For example, "I want to tell you this because this is a huge opportunity to drastically improve your business."

And layer reasons within reasons

Use nested benefit-driven reasons. "I want to tell you this because this information can reduce your expenses by 30%, simplify your production process, and reduce the risk of a bottleneck, so you make more money with less effort because you solved one simple problem."

Use nested urgency-driven reasons. "I want to tell you this because soon it will be too late to act on this information, and I want to make sure you don't miss the chance because we've worked closely for so many years."

Use nested loss-aversion-driven reasons. For example, "I want to tell you this because, without this information, you are significantly more likely to suffer from inefficient production processes, a major leak of wasted resources, and weaker market capitalization because of one pervasive production problem."

Use nested scarcity-driven reasons. For example, "I want to tell you this because nobody else knows it as of now, and you can use it to get a first-mover advantage because the demand is still low, and the price will only rise from here."

Use nested opportunity-driven reasons. For example, "I want to tell you this because this is a huge opportunity to drastically improve your business, simply because it is an untapped market."

Sprinkle reasons everywhere.

They will make you appear drastically more credible.

And while reasons which don't truly justify are still compelling, the best reasons are the real reasons. Find them and explain them.

Frontloaded Transitions: How to Use Attention-Grabbing Transitions and Simple Language Patterns Proven to Quickly Boost Credibility

Let's talk about purpose statements and bridges.

Purpose statements are words, phrases, sentences, paragraphs, etc. that directly contribute to moving the world from where it is to where you want it to be, by manipulating audience cognition.

And manipulating is not a bad word; it simply means deliberately changing.

Bridges, or transitions, smooth the flow of communication by connecting purpose statements.

And they have one particular function: to guarantee that attention is transferred from one statement to the next.

Luckily for you, there's one type of transition that excels at this critical purpose.

I call it a frontloaded transition.

So, how does it work?

It's simple: frontloaded transitions are short phrases that precede a sentence. These are transitions that tease a sentiment that is particularly appealing to people's subconscious biases.

For example, our cognitive machinery sees much of the world as a set of problems and associated solutions. We love solutions. And a frontloaded transition that plays on this is, for example, "Here's the solution…" which teases the sentiment that the solution is coming up, and because people love solutions, they should listen up.

And they do.

But we're talking specifically about credibility.

So, how do frontloaded transitions help you speak with compelling credibility in everyday communication situations?

Here's how: by teasing credible sentiments.

Want some examples?

"Here's the truth…"

"In a spirit of honesty, I tell you this:"

"Here's what they won't tell you:"

"Here's the uncomfortable truth about this:"

"In all honesty…"

"Here's what we're missing:"

"I want to be transparent, so I'll tell you this:"

"If you want the truth, here it is:"

See how these tease sentiments like an honest confession, the truth, or the debunking of a common lie or misconception? See how those are all qualities closely tied to credibility?

These will draw people in.

These will hold attention.

These will convey credibility.

Will they do the trick alone?

No.

Will they help support your other credibility-techniques?

Yes. Tremendously so.

Rhetorical Question Transitions: How to Use a Proven Transition Formula to Command Attention and Portray Credibility

We talked about frontloaded transitions.

Now, let's talk about rhetorical question transitions.

This is not a broad book about the construction of communication content, but specifically about speaking with credibility. So that's why I focus on two of the most compelling transitions instead of giving you all 67 kinds.

So, what are rhetorical question transitions?

Exactly what they sound like: transitions between purpose statements that are rhetorical questions.

Why do they work?

Because they apply the magic of open loops.

And open loops play upon our innate human curiosity.

What's an open loop?

An unanswered question.

That's why so many advertisements for movies end with "will [insert protagonist] achieve [insert goal], or let [insert weaknesses] overcome him?"

There is a gap between what we know and what we want to know, and we'll do anything to fill it. We truly are a curious species.

So, when someone hears "we know that thin capitalization is a problem, but why does it happen?" they tune right in. They want to hear the answer to the question. So they'll listen closely to the speaker.

And just like frontloaded transitions are not inherent credibility boosters, rhetorical questions are not inherently suited to credible communication. But they can be if you engineer credibility-associated sentiments in them.

Let's reengineer our examples of frontloaded transitions into rhetorical question transitions.

"Here's the truth…" becomes "Want to know the truth?"

"In a spirit of honesty, I tell you this:" becomes "In a spirit of honesty, what will I tell you that others won't?

"Here's what they won't tell you:" becomes "What damaging truths will they never tell you?"

"Here's the uncomfortable truth about this:" becomes, "But what's the uncomfortable reality about this?"

"In all honesty…" is difficult to reengineer.

"Here's what we're missing:" becomes "What are we overlooking?"

"I want to be transparent, so I'll tell you this:" becomes "What will a transparent person never hide from you?"

"If you want the truth, here it is:" is difficult to reengineer.

Use these to command undivided attention and earn complete respect when you are speaking, particularly if it is a presentation, speech, or one-way communication situation.

Why use these transitions? Because they gently slide your audience's attention from sentence to sentence instead of losing it.

The Diagnoser Archetype: How to Portray Yourself to Achieve Awe-Inspiring Authority by Applying a Simple, Step-by-Step Strategy

Nearly every single book of mine (all of them so far are on communication) draws a lesson from the same exact moment in our political history.

What's that moment?

When Bill Clinton expressed complete mastery of communication theory in a presidential debate.

I'll spare you the details because you can find the context in all of my other books.

Instead, I'll show you one of the many lessons he taught us in that moment, the one that directly achieves immense credibility in nearly every single situation.

He was responding to this question from an audience member: "How has the national debt personally affected each of your lives and if it hasn't how can you honestly find a cure for the economic problems of the common people if you have no experience in what's ailing them?"

Let's not get into the mistakes his opponent made.

Let's get right into the proven strategy of evoking the diagnoser archetype.

Here's his response (stutters and stumbles included): "Well, I've been governor of a small state for 12 years. I'll tell you how it's affected me personally. Every year, congress - and the president sign laws that makes us - make us do more things and gives us less money to do it with. I see people in my state, middle class people; their taxes have gone up in Washington and their services have gone down, while the wealthy have gotten tax cuts. I have seen what's happened in this last four years, when - in my state, when people lose their jobs there's a good chance I'll know em' by their names. When a factory closes, I know the people who ran it. When the businesses go bankrupt, I know them. And I've been out here for thirteen months, meeting in meetings just like this ever since October, with people like you all over America; people that have lost their jobs, lost their livelihoods, lost their health insurance. What I want you to understand is, the national debt is not the only cause of that. It is because America has not invested in its people; it is because we have not grown; it is because we've had twelve years of trickle-down economics. We've gone from first to twelfth in the world in wages, we've had four years when we produced no private sector jobs, most people are working harder for less money than they were making ten years ago. It is because we are in the grip of a failed economic theory. And this decision you're about to make better be about what kind of economic theory you want; not just people saying I wanna go fix it, but what are we going to do! What I think we have to do is invest in American jobs, American education, control American healthcare costs, and bring the American people together again."

Let's not talk about his brilliant display of genuine empathy.

Let's not talk about his extremely compelling display of authority.

Let's not talk about his highly effective construction of personal ethos.

Let's not talk about his magnitude of evidence.

Let's not talk about his fluency of evidence either.

Let's not talk about his clear, concise, and punchy sentences that grab and hold attention.

Let's not talk about the countless credibility-boosting techniques he uses, or the rhetorical elements of compelling language, or the hundreds of body language and vocal tonality techniques.

No, none of that; though, it's all in there if you can find it.

Let's talk about something that is specifically, deliberately, and intentionally designed to boost credibility in a concise and powerful way.

Here it is: the diagnoser archetype and the structure that evokes it.

Actually, let's call it the *re*diagnoser archetype.

It's simple: he who changes the diagnosis of a problem from an incorrect or incomplete diagnosis to a correct or more complete diagnosis is seen as he who is best equipped to solve the problem, or, in other words, the most credible person in the room.

Get it?

So, how does Clinton do this?

Clinton shifts the diagnosis when he states that "What I want you to understand is, the national debt is not the only cause of that. It is because America has not invested in its people; it is because we have not grown; it is because we've had twelve years of trickle-down economics. We've gone from first to twelfth in the world in wages, we've had four years when we produced no private sector jobs, most people are working harder for less money than they were making ten years ago. It is because we are in the grip of a failed economic theory."

From this speech emerges a simple, step-by-step structure that you can use to instantly achieve immense credibility.

Let's get into it.

Use a brief authority statement (Step one): "Well, I've been governor of a small state for 12 years."

Use a signposting statement that commits to unequivocally answering the implied or (in Clinton's case) explicit question (Step two): "I'll tell you how it's affected me personally."

Use an ethos-statement, conveying your personal connection to the problem, and how it hurts you (Step three): "Every year, congress - and the president sign laws that makes us - make us do more things and gives us less money to do it with. I see people in my state, middle class people; their taxes have gone up in Washington and their services have gone down, while the wealthy have gotten tax cuts. I have seen what's happened in this last four years, when - in my state, when people lose their jobs there's a good chance I'll know em' by their names. When a factory closes, I know the people who ran it. When the businesses go bankrupt, I know them. And I've been out here for thirteen months, meeting in meetings just like this ever since October, with people like you all over America..."

Use a "people's-pain statement" describing the broader pain caused by the problem (Step four): "...people that have lost their jobs, lost their livelihoods, lost their health insurance."

Use a diagnosis-discount statement disconfirming the common diagnosis (Step five): "What I want you to understand is, the national debt is not the only cause of that."

Use a reframing statement presenting your rediagnosis (Step six): "It is because America has not invested in its people; it is because we have not grown; it is because we've had twelve years of trickle-down economics. We've gone from first to twelfth in the world in wages, we've had four years when we produced no private sector jobs, most people are working harder for less money than they were making ten years ago. It is because we are in the grip of a failed economic theory."

Use a solution-presentation statement explaining your solution (Step seven): "And this decision you're about to make better be about what kind of economic theory you want; not just people saying I wanna go fix it, but what are we going to do! What I think we have to do is invest in American jobs, American education, control American healthcare costs, and bring the American people together again."

What's the archetype? There are two parts to it.

Part one: what I call the "doctor" half of the archetype; simply diagnosing a problem lends you credibility in solving it.

Part two: what I call the "visionary" half of the archetype; simply discounting the common consensus as incomplete or shortsighted lends you gravitas and credibility, because you see what most don't.

We could break it up a little further, if we wanted to (and I do!)

Consider the "diagonser" as the one who simply answers the question "why does this problem happen?" and the "rediagnoser" as the one who says "why does this problem happen? It's not what everyone else thinks; it is in fact something else entirely…"

The diagnoser gets an immense amount of credibility.

The rediagnoser gets yet more.

Think about it: the solution which comes from an accurate diagnosis of the problem is that which is most likely to work, right? Obviously. The one who presents an accurate diagnosis is thus seen as the best handler of the problem until someone comes along who rediagnoses the problem and provides a more complete, compelling, insightful, or accurate diagnosis.

There's another psychological principle you must understand: social proof, or our tendency to follow the crowd. You might have realized that rediagnosing necessitates breaking with the crowd, and since people follow the crowd, that turns this psychological principle against you.

Right?

No. At least, not always.

Because think about how Clinton rediagnosed it.

He did not say that the national debt is not a cause of the problem, but that it isn't the *only* cause. He expanded the diagnosis, and the common consensus was not *refuted*, but *built upon* and actually contained within his rediagnoses. This, at the very least, avoids turning social proof against you, and might even turn it on a little.

But one final point.

Since I have introduced you to a structure (communication structures are the focus of my second book, *Effective Communication: The Patterns of Easy Influence*), I must tell you the fundamentals of structure theory.

Use precise tracing. Don't screw around with the structure. It is what it is because it is proven to work; because time and time again, it has produced the desired result. In this case, that is conveying complete credibility. Clinton is not an anecdotal example. I have seen this structure repeated time and time again in countless speeches by people who, in the process, portrayed immense credibility, and have succeeded because of it. So, what do I mean by precise tracing? It's simple: trust the structure and precisely trace it, omitting nothing, and including nothing that's not in it already. Take the structure from beginning to end in a straight line, and do not get wrapped up in tangents and parentheticals. Think of a communication structure as a road, that's specifically designed to get you from point A to point B. In this case, point A is little credibility, and point B is a superabundance of credibility. And it's not just any road, but a narrow bridge, 1,000 feet over white-water rapids down below. It's a thin road. It's easy to deviate from it. There are no barriers stopping you from driving right off it. And it's windy up there on the bridge. **Follow the damn road.** The white-water rapids represent the failed communication that occurs when you stop following the structure. If you decide to use a structure, commit to it. If you decide to get on the bridge, stay on it until the end. This doesn't mean that you must get on the bridge – that you must use a structure – but that when you do, you better follow the structure and precisely trace its steps, doing exactly what they tell you to, nothing less, and nothing more. Get it?

Use separation of concerns. Following the logic of precise tracing, the structure is broken up into sequenced steps for a reason. And what's that reason? The simple fact that this particular sequence of those particular steps is significantly more compelling than these steps in another sequence. Separate your concerns. Do not do step two in step one, or step three in step two, or step one in step five, or… you get the point. Accomplish only the purpose of each step in that step, else the structure falls apart. Bill Clinton didn't do step two after step one and say "I'll tell you how it's affected me personally. Well, I've been governor of a small state for 12 years," which sounds much weaker and less impactful than the correct sequence. There is a place for everything, and everything should be in that place.

Use lengthening. Think of an accordion (I'm full of analogies this chapter, aren't I? First the bridge, now an accordion). Imagine how it compacts and stretches back out again, producing much the same sound in a different pitch and volume. Structures are the same. You can take this structure, and lengthen it to an 80,000-word dissertation. It will have the same impact on a bigger scale.

Use shortening. I'm sure you've already figured this one out. You can compact it. You can make each step just a single sentence. The result? A much quicker, punchier structure that has the same impact on a smaller scale. Get it?

The more and more I study this subject, peeling apart the onion of effective communication, the more and more I realize that structure is more important than I thought. It truly is the key to a new level of fluency in employing the techniques covered in my books, and elsewhere. It makes accessible otherwise difficult and arcane strategies by breaking them down into simple, step-by-step patterns, and organizing them in a specific sequence. I've covered structure to significant depth in *Effective Communication: The Patterns of Easy Influence*, and yet I realize that there is still more depth to be explored. We'll get there soon. :)

Incentive-Bias-Activating If-Then Construction: How to Use a Simple Speaking Pattern to Activate the Incentive-Caused Bias with Ease

An idea in information-exchange theory is called "chunking." Quite simply, chunking posits that people receive and retain information easier in more manageable chunks than in a long, continuous segment. There are a few requirements, such as that each chunk must be built around one key idea. I have a hunch that longer chunks ought to be followed by shorter chunks, to give the mind a break. I know of no scientific literature supporting this, but I'm trusting my gut on this one.

So, to that end, I'm going to give you a shorter chunk now, since we just completed a very long one. :)

Let's get into it.

Remember conditional thinking?

"If X, then Y?"

It is actually an extremely compelling micro-structure; that is, a structure occurring within one sentence.

And remember incentive-caused bias?

That people find more credible that which they want to believe; that which they have an incentive to believe?

Well, this strategy combines incentive-caused bias with if-then conditional language.

It's quite powerful.

All you have to do to use this pattern is say, "if [insert claim] is true, that would mean [insert incentivizing benefits]."

What happens? Those incentivizing benefits make the person want the claim to be true, and so incentive-caused bias works in your favor.

And you can take it to an even more sophisticated level. I vaguely recall the protagonist in the Wolf of Wallstreet (who in real life is actually an incredibly successful sales-coach – Jordan Belfort… you should check out his material) saying "if I am even half right about [insert claim], then that would mean [insert incentivizing benefits]," or more broadly, "if [insert claim] is even [insert fraction of accuracy], then [insert incentivizing benefits]."

Why the "half-right" business? Because the more plausible the claim in the "if [insert claim], then [insert incentivizing benefits]" construction, the more credibility it gleans you, and the less skepticism clouds the incentive-caused bias. And obviously, when we're dealing with probability and chance, the "half-right" qualifier makes it more probable.

Another simple way to apply this is by saying, "if you want [insert benefits], then [insert action]."

I promised you a short chunk, and that's what you got.

Belief Transfer and Mirroring: How to Use a Proven Principle of Human Psychology to Gain the Confidence of Everyone In the Room

You have three languages, remember?

Your words.

Your body language.

Your vocal language.

And, if you want to be a little edgy, the visual aids you might have, like a PowerPoint.

That makes four.

Which language do most of these credibility-boosting techniques fall under?

Your word language.

But not this one. This one directs the proper use of your body language and vocal language to the end of earning the trust and confidence of everyone in the room.

So, what's the strategy?

How do you instantly get everyone's trust and confidence?

How do you exude credibility not with your words but with your body language and vocal tonality?

It's simple: you earn everyone's trust and confidence by applying body language and vocal language that says you have your own trust and your own confidence, both in your abilities and in your ideas.

Before we get into the how, let's discuss the why.

Why do certain patterns of body language and vocal tonality exude immense trust?

Here's why: we can manipulate our words with great ease. It's very easy to say confident words. We can just read them right off of a paper. In other words, we can lie with our words, with great ease. But it's much, much more difficult to lie with our body language and vocal tonality. So, people look to these nonverbal cues to decide whether or not to trust you. And certain use-patterns of these languages are associated with confidence.

Moreover, why is that trust replicated in the minds of your audience members? Why is the trust that you portray in yourself replicated in the minds of your audience? In other words, why is there a belief-transfer?

Three reasons.

Mirroring: people mirror the sentiments they see in those they are with. It's the story every time a grumpy person makes a happy person grumpy, or a happy person makes a grumpy person happy, simply through interacting; it's why waiters and waitresses nod when they say "would you like some dessert?" The table physically mirrors the nodding and then thinks, "oh, I am nodding! That must mean I want dessert." So, your audience has another bias, if it can be called a bias; that in their psychology lies a sleeping giant, a massive lever that you can pull for immense credibility. The lever? Sentiment mirroring. But here's the brutal truth: this lever isn't just "up" or "neutral." It goes all the way from "up" to "*down*," which means that it can work against you too. And if you are not deliberately pushing the lever up, chances are you are accidentally pushing it down. It's why belief-transfer through paralanguage, aka "the nonlexical component of communication by speech, for example, intonation, pitch and speed of speaking hesitation noises, gesture, and facial expression" is so important. How important? That if it is working against you, you are basically ruined. The same words spoken by different speakers, one with confident paralanguage and body language, and one without, receives drastically different reactions. The same words are judged in dramatically different ways simply because of how they are spoken by each speaker. Mirroring is why paralanguage communicating hesitation on your part is replicated by your audience hesitating in believing you. While I don't agree with these proportions, a study once reported that 55 percent of communication is visual (body language), 38 percent is vocal, and only 7 percent is verbal. If they are even half-right (which I believe they are), you would be remiss to leave this credibility-lever untouched. And one final note: mirroring applies with more force with emotional facial expressions and emotional vocal inflections.

Snap categorization: people have preexisting categories in their heads, and when they see a new item (like a new speaker), they snap-categorize them to one of their preexisting categories. Let me explain: people will see quality X in you, see that people in category Y have quality X (in addition to a bundle of qualities Z), and snap categorize you to category Y, thereby inferring that you also have the bundle of qualities Z. This probably explains why the halo effect is so powerful. The halo effect is when one strongly displayed good quality is observed in someone or something, and the observer assigns a halo of unobserved positive qualities to that item. Perhaps snap categorization is the mechanism of the halo effect, where someone portraying the good quality of confidence is snap-categorized to the category of "capable person," and therefore is seen as "smart, driven, and trustworthy," even though they never portrayed those qualities. An example of a category? Capable person is one. So is incapable person. So is smart person. So is credible person. As far as I've heard this concept, I have heard only of one layer of categories. To me, it makes sense that there would be multiple levels of categories, categories within categories, and also that items can belong to multiple categories. But that's beyond the scope of this book. So, what does snap categorization have to do with belief-transfer? It's simple: your body language and vocal language convey one of the first impressions upon which your snap categorization will be based, and therefore confident body language and vocal language will snap categorize you to a category like "credible person," thereby transferring your confidence in your ideas to the observer.

Confidence is self-fulfilling: lastly, belief-transfer works because confidence is self-fulfilling. The person who speaks with calm, controlled confidence likely believes in themselves, and thus will get the damn thing done. Not only that, but people know that your confidence will help you win other people over because it helped win *them* over. They know your confident communication will create belief-transfer with other people as you progress towards your goal, and thus yet more belief-transfer occurs in their minds. They believe you'll get something done because you portray confidence, and they know that your confidence will get yet more people to believe you'll get something done, which will actually make you more likely to get it done. This is closely tied to the credibility-cascade. Remember that?

So, I'm going to tell you exactly how to verbally and nonverbally portray immense self-belief, and thus transfer that belief to your audience and achieve immense credibility.

You must understand the perception-pathways; you must understand nonverbal input and output. You must be able to say to yourself, "if I do X with my body language or vocal language, then that will impact my audience by Y." And not only must you understand cause and effect, but you must be able to actually perform the input correctly.

I'll teach you what to do and how to do it, and I'll give you easy ways to do it correctly, but the only guarantee is practice.

Let's get into it.

Use gentle modulation. Confident people who believe in themselves modulate their voices in gentle, smooth flows, not jagged, rapid, and jarring undulations. Get it? Vocal variation is always a necessity, but when you want to portray unbridled self-confidence, smooth out your vocal variation so that each variation happens slowly; smoothly; instead of so rapidly that it sounds like an out-of-control rollercoaster.

Use contained excitement. Confident people who believe in themselves feel like whatever they are doing might be their big breakthrough. And they know, *know* that it's going to work as intended; they *know* they have it in themselves to seize the moment and achieve their objectives. So, how does this manifest itself in a voice? With contained excitement. Think about it: confident people think whatever they're doing is their next big opportunity. They think this is their shot at making it big. Obviously, they should be excited about it. But it must be excitement that is just bubbling under the surface. It must be excitement under the reigns of an objective, logical, and controlled mind; a mind that is poised and patient.

Use hypophora. This one technique is actually not vocal or body-language, though our coming addition to it will be. If you recall, hypophora is simply asking a question and then answering it yourself. Questions work for many reasons: they are open loops, they are scientifically proven to be more memorable, and they grab attention. The human mind likes questions. The human mind interacts effortlessly with questions. And asking a question mirrors the uncertainty some people might be feeling, while answering the question expresses your confidence cutting through the confusion with a clear answer. "Why does this happen? Because…" "But what can we do about it? The first step…" "So, what does this mean for us? That…"

Use the precise-analysis tonality. I call this the precise-analysis tonality because coupled with hypophora (a word-language technique), it is extremely compelling and produces the undeniable perception of confidence. How does it work? Well, remember breaking rapport tonality and open rapport tonality? Open rapport tonality is when the pitch goes up at the end of a sentence. It signals that it is a question; it is associated with uncertainty, with impromptu and questionable rumination, with imprecise confusion. But it grabs attention and signals the start of rapport: the start of two-way communication. And breaking rapport tonality signals the breaking off of rapport, conclusion, confidence, clarity, and the perception that what you are saying needs no validation. Breaking rapport is achieved by lowering your pitch at the end of a sentence. So, how do you combine open rapport tonality and breaking rapport tonality with hypophora? It's simple: apply open rapport to the question, and then breaking rapport to the answer. This is a brilliant strategy for achieving confident communication, and therefore credibility by belief-transfer because it makes you seem sharp, well-researched, perceptive, and analytical.

Use a slower pace. Nine times out of ten, a nervous speaker will speak quickly, unleashing a rapid-fire barrage of poorly enunciated, wavering words onto the perplexed audience. Why do they do that? Why do they speak quickly? Because they want to sit down. They want to leave the limelight. They don't want to be the center of attention anymore. They want to escape the stage, which is the source of their nervousness. So, do the opposite. Get up there, and speak slowly; with precision; with enunciation; with controlled pace, and deliberate articulation that signals to everyone that you are methodical and willing to be in the limelight for as long as you need to be. Not to mention that talking slower makes it easier for others to hear you, and easier for you to apply deliberate modulation.

Use emphasized absolutes. What sounds more confident? "This might possibly be the best opportunity given the right circumstances," or "this is the best possible opportunity?" Definitely the last one. Why? Because it uses absolutes: not "this could be," but "this is." Not "I think this might be," but "this is." Not "It appears to me that…" but "The truth is that…" Assert yourself. Assert your ideas. Assert your analysis. And do it with absolutes. But that's a word-language technique, so why is it here? Because, like hypophora, it calls upon one other technique for added impact. That technique? Emphasis. What is emphasis? This is the simple definition: using your vocal modulation to provide extra importance to a word. "This is the solution" becomes "THIS IS the solution." So, step one is to rephrase unclear, unassertive, weak sentences into ones that are based around absolutes. And then step two is to emphasize the absolutes. How? It is probably natural to you already. But if not, here's how: to emphasize a word, say the first syllable slightly louder than the other words in the sentence, make the pitch of the word either higher or lower (I recommend lower) than the other words in the sentence, say it slower than you normally would, stretch the vowel sound, and make a brief pause after you say it. And, as always, use your body to express the same sentiment as your voice; if you want to emphasize a word, do so with accompanying gestures as well.

Use upper-facial positioning. What seems more confident to you, someone who is looking down, or someone who tilts their head ever-so-slightly up? Someone who tilts their head up. This indicates that you are not afraid to be seen, which evokes confidence. Don't over-tilt it; just a gentle nudge up.

Use precise gestures. Confidence and control are so closely associated that one almost always indicates the presence of the other. Precise gestures are controlled; they are closely tied to your words; they are smooth, and they do not include anything unintentional. They are tied to your words because they mirror the flow of your modulation. For example, are you emphasizing the three big ideas in a proposal? Chances are, you are providing verbal emphasis on the "first… second… third…"

signposts. Do it with your gestures too. How? I'll give you an example. Take your right hand and touch your right shoulder. Twist your hand 90 degrees to the left. Extend your arm at the elbow until the angle between your upper arm and your forearm is about 45 degrees. Extend your fingers and moderately tense up your hand. Don't have T-Rex arms; keep everything the same, but unglue your elbow from your side, if it is taped up against it. Then when you say "first," from this position, jut out your hand decisively and rapidly, but ever-so-slightly. Do the same for "second" and "third." Every new number, move the gesturing-point of the hand an inch lower. This is a precise, punchy gesture that delineates the items in your list.

Use extreme breaking-rapport. We talked about the impacts of breaking rapport. But here's what you need to know: the greater the breaking rapport (in other words, the lower the pitch drops at the end of a sentence), the greater the sense of conclusion becomes. And breaking rapport is not limited to pitch, but projection and pace too. Your PPP qualities (projection, pace, and pitch) should start where they are natural, then rise through the middle of the sentence, and come back down at the end; a gentle hill, like a normal probability distribution.

Use conviction-transitions. Conviction transitions were one of my favorite tools back in my competitive debating days (my opponents all hated me for using all these techniques and winning over and over because of it). What is a conviction-transition? It couples emphatic vocal modulation with a clump of words that delivers confidence and clarity. For example, after providing some evidence, a conviction-transition would be "What this unequivocally proves, beyond the shadow of a single doubt, is that..." Transitions connect what you just said to what you are about to say, and conviction-transitions embed in that connection a sense of undeniable truth, of unequivocal reality. Other examples are "What we know for sure is that..." "What is abundantly clear to us based on the massive mountain of evidence is that..." "What we can't deny is the obvious fact that..." The basic pattern is "What is [insert list of qualities portraying complete confidence] is that [insert statement]." So, what about the vocal element of this? Well, there's a certain type of tonality that, even after all these years writing on this subject and teaching it to others, I have a hard time explaining on paper. It's sort of a power-voice; it's a rasp, a forceful inflection; it has force, potency, almost like a loud whisper, like you are employing the energy of your entire body to say this thing that you are going to say, but you also want to restrain it at the same time. It emanates from deep inside of you and engages your entire speaking apparatus. I've heard it called a power-whisper before. Apply this tonality to your conviction-transitions. And sprinkle some magic conviction-words in the transitions (and elsewhere, if you'd like). I love "What this undeniably, unequivocally, and unambiguously proves" because of the tricolon, the micro-repetition, the scesis onomaton, the alliteration, the "ly" rhyming, the flow, the assonance, and the assertive, confident meaning.

Use lower depth. It's simple, and it's silly, but it's true, and you should do it if you can: speaking with a lower depth gives you gravitas, grandeur, and the perception of complete confidence. It has to do with the ancient pathways in our minds. We just associate a lower depth with more confidence. But take two versions of the same exact statement, and have someone with a deep voice speak it, versus someone with a higher-pitched voice. The depth gives it so much more strength. It portrays much, much more confidence, for no rational reason whatsoever. If you've been following recent politics (that is 2019-2020 Democratic primary politics), you've heard candidate Pete Buttigieg speak, and you've heard his baritone voice that makes everything he says sound more confident. The same is true of Bernie Sanders and Barack Obama. Especially Obama.

Use stumble-free flow. Let me tell you the truth: stumbles are not the problem. Reacting to them poorly is. Accept stumbles if they come, do not panic, recollect yourself with the understanding that nobody cares if you stumble, and continue with confidence. That said, to prevent them, do the following: know your content, have it in your mind, not on paper (looking back-and-forth at the paper is the source of countless stumbles), speak slowly, think one sentence ahead, lift your inhibitions and focus on the meaning you want to impart.

Use sentence-remapping. What are conversation fillers? Phrases like "uh, um, like, and you know" that fill your conversation. Why do they do this? Why do they constantly pop into our speech? Because our brains tell themselves something like this: "Right now I am speaking, when I am speaking I must be making sound, if I am not making sound that means something I will compensate by making sound that doesn't mean anything but is still sound, because then I will at least be making sound, which is what I'm supposed to do when I'm speaking, and right now, I am in a state of speaking." And this is a difficult process to override, but it becomes easier over time if you watch yourself; be like an attentive guard watching out for conversation fillers. Accept them if they come, but be aware of how often and when you use them. Simply take your awareness of your conversation fillers, and move it from your subconscious mind to your conscious mind. Once you pay conversation fillers notice, they slowly slide back out of your speech just as easily as they first slid in, simply because you mentally preempt them, planting an actual word or a pause where a conversation filler would have occured. And that's critical too: a pause is infinitely, dramatically, drastically better than a conversation filler. Just pause. And slow down, so you can feel the conversation fillers coming, and react with more ease and fluency. But let's talk about sentence-remapping, because it works. So, what is it? Well, I'll explain: when you are speaking, you often *plan* your next sentence. In other words, you have your next sentence booted up and ready to launch in your mind. So, you start speaking it. Let's say it was, "And that's why we should vote for a Republican in 2020." You say, "And that's why…" which is great so far, but then "they" instead of "we." You accidentally deviated from your plan. Nine times out of ten, this is where a stumble or conversation filler will occur, and a mistake that blurs your clarity (though it is by no means the end of the world). Specifically, the person will probably say, "and that's why they- uh, um, *we*- should vote for a Republican in 2020." But sentence-remapping does something else. It alters the plan to flow with the mistake, thereby removing the conversation filler and stumble. How? For example, like this: "and that's why they, …*(ditch the original plan and reform the planned sentence to flow with the mistake)*… the Republican party, should get the support of our votes and voices in 2020." See how the sentence is remapped to flow with the mistake instead of sticking to a plan that you deviated from? It all comes down to this: don't go back to satisfy the plan you had, go forward with a new plan. Some people do this automatically and naturally. Some people need specific practice in this technique. But it is a powerful one nonetheless.

Use sentence-chains. We'll talk about this later, but one of the most common confidence-ruining fears is your mind going blank when you're in front of everyone. Think about it. It's pretty scary, right? You have a brilliant set of ideas to share, but then they get vacuumed out of your mind, leaving it empty right as you claim the floor. 20 seconds pass. You've said nothing. 30. 40. A minute. Two minutes. You excuse yourself. Scary, right? No, not at all. Don't listen to this part of your brain. And realize that all you have to do to instantly have content to share with your audience is to apply the sentence-chain principle. It's easy: pick the single most important thing you want to say, summarize it in one or a few sentences, say it, and then simply chain the rest of your communication off of that. Simply say *something*, and build your next something off of the first something. This forms a continuous chain of fluent, natural sentences, simply because one leads to the other. By having a sentence behind you to build your next one on, you give your mind the necessary stimulus to quickly and fluently produce the content you want to share. Simple, but effective.

Use confidence-words and confidence-phrases. I promised you vocal and body language techniques, but these words and phrases are just too important. Bear with me here. There are some words that communicate uncompromising confidence in your abilities, your analysis, and your ideas. Some examples? "Self-evident, doubtlessly, completely, dramatically, drastically," are just some. Sprinkle these words throughout your communication to appear more confident. It's simple and easy, but effective.

Use planted feet. When people lack confidence, they will do one of two things very frequently: rapidly shift their body weight from foot to foot, or walk forward and backward over and over again. None of that madness. None of it. Plant your two feet, and do not move unless you do so for a deliberate, intentional purpose, such as moving to another side of the room to engage people closer to that side. Trust me on this. People say they do it because planting their feet in a position and not moving them around would make them seem stiff. That's not true at all, though, and it's also not the real reason they do it. They do it because they are incredibly nervous, *which is okay.* But minimize the impacts of it if you can. How? By planting your two feet, which communicates that complete control and confidence instead of nervous energy is the state of your mind.

Use mid-ground projection. What's this? Simply put, this is the highest volume at which you can use your *talking* voice. Speak not like a grand orator in the Roman Senate, but like you would talk to a professional contact in a very loud restaurant. You'd talk much louder, but you wouldn't yell; find the line where you go from speaking to shouting, and go right up to it, but not on it, and no further than this point.

The Feel, Felt, Found Model: How to Apply a Proven, Guaranteed, Step-by-Step Structure to Instantly Handle an Objection with Ease

What if all you had to do to drastically improve the efficacy of your persuasion, influence, and communication, was to implement one simple strategy? If you haven't gotten this by now, when I say "what if [insert awesome thing] is real," it usually is. So, let's get into the mind-blowing strategy of pacing and leading, which works with surprising reliability.

Credible communication is leading people to your point of view by getting them to believe you. But if you want to lead people, show them that you can match their pace first. Why? Because people have a natural aversion to being led, it's called persuasion aversion, and this one simple function of the human mind thwarts much of our persuasive communication.

So, what does this actually mean? This: instead of getting straight into asserting your position and speaking your mind (leading), echo the sentiment of your audience's position, and speak your audience's mind (pacing). Get it?

Let's say, in an incredibly simple example, that your audience's position is "X is bad," and your position is "X is good." There are two ways you can go about this, and one is drastically more effective, yet sadly less common. Here they are: first, leading: "X is good." Second, pacing and leading: "I hear what you're saying, honestly... X has [insert bad characteristic], and [insert bad characteristic two]. It can be frustrating when X makes us feel [insert negative emotion]. Trust me; I get it. X is also [insert good characteristic one], and [insert good characteristic two]. One time, I was struggling with [insert unrelated struggle], and it was X that helped me out. All in all, X isn't so bad. X is good."

When you psychologically assault people with an opposing point of view (which I call psychological assault because the areas of the brain that light up during physical assault light up in an argument too), they are immediately entrenched, ready for war. But when you start by pacing, you prevent them from jumping into their mental trenches and pulling out their cognitive disconfirmation guns. And when you slowly side from pacing them to leading them, *they don't even realize what is happening*, and never have time to jump into their trenches, on the defensive. On the contrary, they feel affirmed, and people who feel affirmed are more willing to affirm. They feel open and more receptive to your ideas, all because you showed them the same courtesy, and they feel that they are heard and their opinions valued.

Now, for the first of our guidelines, don't use a word like "but," "yet," "still," "though," etc. Why? Because, what do those words do? They signal a discounting of what you just said; in other words, a discounting of the pacing. And that ruins it. Try to slide from pacing to leading without using one of these words. It's tricky, but check out the example on the last page. Don't worry if you use one of these discounter words: it's not the end of the world.

For the second of our guidelines, and as a testament to the value of pacing and leading, you must remember this: pacing works even if the other person is not opposed, but neutral. If they are unsure, you can pace their uncertainty. In other words: if people are [insert any quality one] about a subject, whether it is uncertain, angry, or opposed, then you can pace that quality before leading them to [insert any quality two], whether that is certain, relaxed, or in agreement. But quality two does not have to be a converse of quality one. You can pace from any starting point, and lead to any ending point.

Pacing and leading brings us to a general rule: the halo effect strikes again. In other words: however, people feel about the beginning of your communication is how they are likely to feel about the end of it, even if the end contradicts the start in sentiment. And pacing and leading guarantees that they will feel good about the start, thus better about the end.

And you need to strike a balancing act. Let's say you're pacing and leading from "X is bad" to "X is good." If you pace too much, excessively affirming and reaffirming "X is bad," any leading is weakened, and the starting sentiment is strengthened. On the contrary, if you pace too little, the whole thing falls apart; leading is weakened then too because the pacing has not yet taken effect, and the entire scheme seems disingenuous. The same is true if you lead too little. So, you must strike a balance: pace enough so that it takes the effect of opening someone's mind, not so much that it takes the effect of further entrenching their original opinion; and lead enough so that it takes the effect of imparting your point of view, but not so much that its weight crumbles the whole scheme.

This previous paragraph can be summarized in this sentence: make your pacing and leading gradual, gentle, and *honest*. And before we move on, remember the broader wisdom of pacing and leading: if you want to prove a man wrong in such a way that he admits it, start by telling him he's right.

So, what is the feel, felt, found model? It's brilliant. And I give credit where credit is due: I discovered it in an Earl Nightingale publication. I highly recommend all the Nightingale-Conant publications. They are extremely valuable. The feel, felt, found model is a simple, step-by-step pattern that is highly memorable for you, that instantly handles audience objections with pacing and leading.

First, in response to an objection, you say, "I feel the same way. [Insert echoing of audience beliefs. Repeat their objection back to them]." Then, you say, "A lot of people felt the same way too." And finally, you conclude with "Until they found that [insert objection nullification]."

See the immense power of the feel, felt, found method? See how it uses pacing and leading in an insanely effective way?

Now, most people would make one big mistake.

The mistake? To start with nullifying their objection.

But now that you know all about pacing and leading, you understand exactly why starting with the nullification is not only ineffective but actually feels aggressive to your audience members. You know that when someone's intellectual status quo is threatened, they put up walls so tough that, in some cases, no amount of truth, evidence, or logic can break them down. But with pacing and leading? You build bridges, not walls. Affirm them, and they shall affirm you.

There's a smart saying.

Here it is: The first words you should say when trying to convince someone they're wrong, are "you're right."

Think about it.

Remember it.

Apply pacing and leading with the feel-felt-found method which stems from it.

The Clarity Principle: How to Avoid the Biggest, Most Confusing Speaking Mistake People Always Make Without Even Realizing it

He who is not clear is not credible. That feels fairly obvious, right? It should be.

But I'm not in the business of giving obvious advice.

So, what am I going to tell you this chapter?

I'm going to tell you not to be clear (that's shallow and trite), but the two biggest clarity-reducing mistakes you must understand and avoid like the plague.

They will completely derail your communication and drastically undermine your credibility.

They will ruin your chances of portraying confidence in your ideas and self.

They will confuse your audience members and make communication anxiety more pronounced as you find yourself in a tangle of muddy, blurry, unclear thoughts.

What are the two credibility killers you must avoid?

Avoid parentheticals. When you are writing, go ahead and write longer sentences that wind about and include little folds, ideas in parenthesis, ideas delineated by dashes – like this – and semicolons; whatever suits your fancy. It's okay when you're writing. Why? Because your audience members – in this case, readers – can easily slow down the flow of communication to make it more manageable. In other words, they control the rate of information exchange: they can slow down, they can reread, they can break it up into parts, they can read it five times if they want, whatever. Now, this is not ideal, but it's not going to kill your writing. However, it will kill your spoken communication like nothing else. Why? Because when you are speaking, think about the flow of information exchange: short of raising their hands and interrupting you to ask a question or to prompt a repetition, your audience members have no control over the rate of information exchange. They either match it or don't, and the moment the rate exceeds their information absorption capabilities, they give up and check out. You are simply speaking with too much complexity; so much of it that it exceeds what listeners can reasonably comprehend. And even if they could comprehend it, remember the marginal net gain model: by adding unnecessary complexity, you are raising percieved (and real) marginal costs of listening to you.

So, a sentence like this one, one that has twists and turns – even without big words – and a sentence which extends itself (and includes side-thoughts and related anecdotes in parenthesis) but doesn't concisely center on one idea, possibly including examples of many different ideas under the roof of one sentence, though not tying them back to one – or perhaps two (but not three) – major thematic element or, in the case of more examples, elements plural, won't kill your writing.

It will only bring your writing to the brink of death.

It's so incredibly far from ideal writing.

But a reader can comprehend it, with a little boost of added effort.

A listener, however, would get lost.

Why?

Because of all the twists and turns embedded in that sentence.

All the tangents.

All the parentheticals.

All the added pieces of relevant but unnecessary details.

All the rumination.

All the content that is not tied to one central idea.

All the meta-information, or information about information.

All the superabundance of nonsense.

Those things can be overcome by a moderately persistent reader, but even the most persistent listener would lose you around "and includes side-thoughts and related anecdotes in parenthesis."

You are simply providing so much information that is unnecessary, and at a rate, they can't match with their information intake.

So, want to maintain clarity in your communication? Short, punchy, decisive sentences that flow off the tongue at the rate in which your audience's ears can capture them.

Much rhetorically beautiful language (like JFK's, which I love to analyze) includes some longer sentences. But only after earning attention with shorter, easy sentences; and even those longer sentences do not try to take on more than they can handle by using a complex structure. They are long, but the micro-structures embedded in the language breaks up information in such a way that longer sentences are easier to grasp.

So, what is a parenthetical?

It's not as black and white in speaking as it is in writing.

I think of it like this: a parenthetical is an attempt by the speaker to include a sub-point or sub-message in a sentence with a different purpose entirely.

But that's not a good idea.

And often, a parenthetical is information about information, or meta-information.

Each sentence should have one purpose, accomplish it quickly, decisively, and effortlessly, and then include the sub-point or sub-message in the next sentence if it is so important.

Give each sentence a job, do that job in that sentence, and no other job. Leave the rest to the other sentences.

Avoid tangents. Here's when tangents happen: we are speaking a sentence with a clear purpose (whether we realize the purpose or not), we get another idea that flashes into our head, and we jump on that idea, deviating the path of the sentence and not achieving a synthesis of the original thought. We say something like "and, by the way…" or "which, if we think about it…" and then we deliver that new idea instead of the first one, which we interrupted.

The man who chases two rabbits catches neither.

So, it's already bad at this point; it's already bad the moment you deviate from the precise path of a sentence to stuff in another idea.

But it gets worse when we forget to close the original sentence and leave a loose end up in the air.

Want some examples?

Here's a sentence with no tangent: "Denmark is not a good economic model for the United States because it is 1/60th of the size."

Here's a sentence with a tangent that loops back around into the original sentence: "Denmark is not a good economic model for the United States because – by the way, it has its own sct of problems that we shouldn't be praising so highly – not to mention, though, that it is 1/60th of the size."

Here's a sentence with a tangent that concludes without looping back into the original sentence: "Denmark is not a good economic model for the United States because – by the way, it has its own set of problems that we shouldn't be praising so highly as virtually every single nation does that we seem to ignore when using it as a praiseworthy economy to replicate."

It gets worse. And I've seen this happen to people before.

Or rather, I've seen them do this to themselves.

They'll make a tangent off of a tangent: "Denmark is not a good economic model for the United States because – by the way, it has its own set of problems that we shouldn't be praising so highly as virtually every single nation does that we seem to ignore when using it as a praiseworthy economy to replicate, which is no different than the United States, not to mention their nonexistent need to protect half of Europe with their military, like we do, which is why we can't have the social services they have."

Let me annotate this with exactly what's going on in the speaker's head, in one form or another: "*(Tell them about how Denmark's size makes any comparison unrealistic)* Denmark is not a good economic model for the United States because – *(Oh wait! Also mention how, even if it was a realistic comparison, it wouldn't be something we'd want to replicate)* by the way, it has its own set of problems that we shouldn't be praising so highly, *(But make sure that they know it's not just Denmark that has problems)* as virtually every single nation does, *(You're losing control of this thought… what were you talking about? Oh right, that we ignore the problems with economies we try to replicate)* that we seem to ignore when using it as a praiseworthy economy to replicate *(And make sure they know that we are not unique as a country)*, which is no different than the United States, *(That's right! The United States! You were talking about the United States, right? How did you get here? Bring it back… uhh how though? NATO! Military alliances is a good turning point back…)* not to mention their nonexistent need to protect half of Europe with their military, like we do *(But you were going to say they have social services that we can't have…)*, which is why we can't have the social services they have."

Simplicity is eloquence, and eloquence is credibility.

We already talked about the aesthetic impact bias, right?

Anyway, how would we rephrase that sentence? Well, it's simple, and it's *necessary*, and it's drastically and dramatically better than the tangent-filled version.

You need two things to avoid this.

What are the two things?

Discipline is the first.

Memory is the second.

First, have the discipline to think to yourself, "Wait! This thought, while great, doesn't belong here. It will get its own sentence as soon as I complete the synthesis of this thought I'm currently on."

Then, have the memory to think to yourself, "Alright! I finished that thought. Now, what was that other one I had mid-sentence? Oh right… I got it! Let's deliver it now."

That means finishing the thought you're on and postponing the tangential thought to the next sentence. Which would turn that mess into this: "Denmark is not a good economic model for the United States because it is 1/60th of the size. And it has its own set of problems that we shouldn't be praising so highly. Virtually every single nation does. And we seem to ignore problems when using an economy as a praiseworthy model. They are no different and have problems, just like the United States. But Denmark does not need to protect half of Europe with its military. We do. This is why we can't have the social services they have."

This is how some lucky few of us can speak fluently for 20-30 minutes at a time about complex subjects. We have a sentence, we start it, we get a thought mid-sentence, and we postpone it to the next sentence. And we now have something to say next. But when we're saying this next thing, we get another thought, getting bumped to another sentence, and yet again another thought during that next sentence. This is the essence of sentence-chaining.

Why are we so tempted to jump into the tangent instead of finishing the thought we are on?

A few reasons, in my belief: namely that a thought is fleeting. We don't want to miss it. We don't want to file it away but lose it when we need to draw it back out. And also, we're so used to not having a flow of fluent thoughts when we're nervous that if we do have such a flow, it's tempting to let it go unbridled.

But reign it in.

Control it.

Put the tangent in its place.

And by avoiding parentheticals and tangents, you will become infinitely more credible.

Or, rather, you'll avoid becoming more and more undermined by confusing people every time you speak.

This won't necessarily make you credible; it will just avoid the single situation that will vacuum up all of your credibility: a confused audience.

And even worse... a confused you.

Event Recollection: How to Persuade Your Audience with a Trojan-Horse Technique That Works Without Fail, Every Single Time

I was talking to a friend who was involved in operating the apparatus of a national political campaign devoted to whipping up votes, support, and donations from my state.

He told me something interesting.

He said that when canvassing (going door-to-door to help undecided voters come to the obviously correct conclusion that they should vote for your candidate), you have to use a particular strategy.

I was fascinated, and this confirmed a long-term hunch of mine.

It also evoked an image of a Trojan Horse.

The Trojan Horse (a personal story) was how the Greek military (your persuasive ideas) invaded the impervious walls of Troy (your audience's persuasion resistance); they built a giant wooden horse, and stuck a small squadron of Greek soldiers in it, before offering it as an olive-branch to Troy.

The Trojans took it in without realizing what was contained in it.

And it is because of this that what was contained in it – the Greek soldiers – managed to take the city from within, after years of brutal combat from outside the walls.

Let me explain the canvassing strategy.

What do you not do?

Go in there and say, "Here's why you should vote for this candidate."

That's the intuitive image of persuasion we assume goes down in these door-to-door meetings.

And that's what the Greeks were doing for years before they got the Trojan Horse idea.

But it's not how it works.

The better strategy is to do something different entirely. Something that embeds the elements of persuasion in the sneaky, subtle facade of a personal story.

So, instead of saying, "here's why you should vote for this candidate," you're supposed to say, "I was once undecided myself. The reason I am now a supporter of this candidate is that..." and tell the story of your conversion from undecided to decided.

Get it?

It is a form of pacing and leading.

It activates the intuitive bias.

It activates countless functions of human psychology that we discussed, all in your favor.

It is gentle, and gentle persuasion builds credibility, while overt and aggressive persuasion destroys it.

It fosters likeability, and people find those they like much more credible.

It is conversational and promotes two-way communication, which is attention-grabbing. Attention is a prerequisite for credibility.

In short, the strategy is this: embedding persuasive elements in a personal story.

Either "I used to believe X, and now I believe Y, because..."

Or, "One time I [insert personal story]. This was when I realized that [insert what you want them to believe]."

And even, "I used to be a fervent opponent of X, but after I had a particular moment that I will never forget, I realized that maybe it wasn't so bad all along. What happened was [insert personal story]."

The stories should be personal and should foster a connection between you and your audiences.

This is always true: first connect, then persuade.

That is not merely a *better* way.

It is the *only* way.

And what better method to build a genuinely powerful connection than to tell a related personal story that truly is personal, maybe even a little emotional?

And what better way to build credibility than to embed in this personal story the exact reasons why your audience members should believe you?

There is no better way: trust me on that.

This strategy is proven to work; proven to build credibility; proven to empower connections that change minds.

Use it.

Use Ruminating Delivery: How to Appear Completely Authentic With One Simple Strategy That Instantly Simplifies Communication

What do former President Barack Obama and Democratic presidential candidate Pete Buttigieg have in common?

They are both incredible public speakers.

Truly phenomenal ones.

And they also both appear completely authentic by applying one particularly effective mode of delivery.

This strategy works its charming magic on nearly everyone, save for those dramatically opposed to their political stances.

So, what's the strategy?

Well, let me tell you what it feels to listen to these two. Maybe you'll pick up on the strategy they use while I'm explaining the experience of listening to them.

It feels like they are saying exactly what they are thinking.

It feels like they are slowly turning the subject matter over in their heads.

It feels like they are applying their intellectual energies right there in front of you, in the moment, trying to uncover the hidden truth and embedded logic of whatever it is they are speaking about.

When they say something, to me at least, it evokes the same sense as a freshly printed paper coming out of the printer, nice and warm.

It seems like they just discovered something after ruminating on it for a few minutes, and want to share it in its early stages.

And yet they do this without seeming unprepared.

So, what's the strategy?

Well, I just said it: ruminating delivery.

It is a proven method for achieving authenticity.

It is a proven method for creating credibility.

It is a proven method for changing minds and influencing people by making them trust you, what you say, and what you represent.

How does it work?

Quite simply, it is a mode of delivery (that is, a clump of vocal modulation and body language techniques) that makes it seem like these people are ruminating on a subject right there before our very eyes, and then giving us what pops into their heads, with no filter.

They make themselves seem deep in thought.

And when they do that, we are intrigued.

Suspense builds.

Attention increases.

Intensity heightens.

"What is this person thinking about? What are they going to say? Come on! Get it out. I'm interested."

Think about it: hate them or love them, these two people (and many others who use this strategy) are very intelligent.

That's indisputable.

And when a very intelligent person with a history of personal ethos and credibility is up there, deep in thought, you naturally want to know what that session of deep thought produces.

But don't get me wrong: grabbing and holding attention in a subtle yet powerful way is not the main function of this strategy.

What is, then?

Building authenticity.

So, why does it do that?

It sounds like it's not prepared.

It makes direct communication yet more direct.

It makes it feel like a closer connection between speaker and audience because the speaker is delivering the thoughts the moment they are produced by their deep-thinking session, in the exact way they were phrased in their mind.

Again, just like a freshly printed first-draft manuscript off the press.

It is the *first* draft.

It is not dressed up.

It is not built upon by iteration after iteration of improvement cycles.

It is honest, even if a little flawed.

But how do they actually signal this?

How do they create the impression of deep thought?

It is very, very subtle, so subtle that it demands an immense amount of control over voice and body, and it is also fleeting: they are not up there for hours thinking through the problem, only for a few seconds before speaking.

Obama seemed to do it by narrowing his eyes, pausing, looking off to the side, often a little towards the sky, putting on a facial expression of thoughtful effort as though his mental effort was actually straining his facial muscles, then looking at his audience, and delivering the beautifully-worded and eloquently-delivered first-draft result of this deep-thought session.

Buttigieg does it by tilting his head slightly down, pausing (which is necessary for this strategy), putting on the sort of frown that is not the result frustration, but effortful thinking, and then curtly smiling as if he just had a light-bulb moment, at which point he slowly ramps back up into speaking.

Now, I could break it down yet further.

But the best way to truly understand how these speakers achieve ruminating delivery is to watch them speak. Just go to YouTube, type in "Buttigieg speech" or "Obama speech," and watch one.

You'll see exactly what they do.

Difficulty, Discovery, Decision Trifecta: How to Use a Hidden, Little-Known Structure that Combines Dozens of Strategies

I've said it before, and I'll say it again.

The more I study this subject, the more I realize what it so often comes down to: structure, structure, structure.

Structured communication is so incredibly brilliant in its efficacy and ease of use.

Structured communication makes these strategies so much more accessible.

Structured communication becomes more than the sum of its parts, simply by virtue of organizing them in a sequence.

I wrote my entire second book on structure, and yet I keep realizing that there's more to it.

How can you effortlessly incorporate a carefully selected, synergistic handful of these strategies into a single piece of communication?

Structure.

How can you instantly simplify communication and make it much more fluent to deliver?

Structure.

How can you guarantee that your persuasive power and credibility are maximized?

Structure.

So, I want to show you a structure that came to me recently. It is specifically designed to build belief; to create credibility.

It's called the difficulty, discovery, decision trifecta.

And the theory behind it is complicated.

Which doesn't mean that I will omit the theory, but that I will place particular emphasis on it.

So, let's get into why this trifecta structure works, before we get into what it is, and how to execute it.

This will have us calling upon psychological biases and cognitive tendencies once more.

First, we know that people tend towards doubt avoidance. When we feel doubt, we feel discomfort, and when we feel discomfort, we want to escape it. If the discomfort is caused by doubt, we escape the discomfort by procrastinating the decision or jumping to a premature decision. Two kinds of people are dominated by this dynamic: indecise people (not making decisions) and impulsive people (making decisions too quickly). The rest of this approach will ensure that procrastination doesn't happen, but that decision does. Know this: people will usually try to escape the discomfort caused by doubt by going with the first decision they see before them.

So, what happens then?

What happens when they do that?

They become entrenched in it.

Why? Because of the endowment effect (what is theirs is viewed as more valuable, including a decision) and inconsistency avoidance (what is inconsistent with their past actions, they avoid, and what is consistent with them, they are drawn to).

See how this comes together?

Now, the strategy is this: first, present difficulty that creates doubt, then present a discovery that eases the doubt, and then, use the combined force of the psychological factors thus far activated to present a much more attractive decision which much more credibility.

Get it?

So, how do you create difficulty and doubt in the first place?

There are many ways, but for simplicity's sake, I'll give you three. They are all you really need at this point.

Use conflicting social proof. People follow the crowd. It is such an insanely powerful tendency that it is the predominant cause for many of our actions, whether we realize it or not. But what if the crowd is going in two opposite directions? What if you present social proof that does nothing but expose the lack of social consensus? What if you express the debate between the two camps, diving deep into the reasons why each believes what they believe?

Use conflicting evidence. Present two pieces of evidence that suggest different conclusions and uncertainty will ensue. Present one piece of evidence that suggests one conclusion, and another that suggests the opposite conclusion.

Use conflicting authorities. Present two experts vehemently, even viciously asserting opposite conclusions.

Do you see what you're doing?

You're creating certainty by first creating uncertainty.

Why? Because people who are uncertain want to reach a point of certainty more than people who are not uncertain. People do not feel compelled to reach a decision and dispel the doubt if there is no doubt. And if there is no doubt that your proposal is the best one, there's no need to quickly reach a certain decision.

In other words, certainty is more attractive in the context of uncertainty.

Contrast strikes again.

So does context.

These are the same reasons a solution is more attractive in the context of the problem it solves.

The structure is, stripped down to its bare essentials, this: "Here are the reasons this is a difficult question that creates doubt, here is the discovery I made that dispels the doubt, and here is the conclusion that this discovery supports."

Don't paralyze them with doubt.

You must guarantee that the weight of your discovery overpowers the doubt you created.

Create just enough doubt that there is doubt for them to escape.

Create just enough doubt that they want to make a quick decision to feel their treasured certainty again.

Create just enough doubt that they treasure your doubt-dispelling discovery.

Opposition Kindness: How to Avoid the Single Most Damaging, Credibility-Destroying Mistake People Are Always Making

The hidden, little-known secrets of powerful communication expose themselves in the words of legendary communicators.

So, what secret does this following excerpt expose?

I'll let you find it on your own before telling you. Hint: the title of this section is "opposition kindness."

These words were spoken by Frederick Douglas.

"Fellow Citizens, I am not wanting in respect for the fathers of this republic. The signers of the Declaration of Independence were brave men. They were great men, too great enough to give frame to a great age. It does not often happen to a nation to raise, at one time, such a number of truly great men. The point from which I am compelled to view them is not, certainly, the most favorable; and yet I cannot contemplate their great deeds with less than admiration. They were statesmen, patriots and heroes, and for the good they did, and the principles they contended for, I will unite with you to honor their memory…"

Did you find the strategy?

Here it is: Frederick Douglas, instead of violently, vehemently, and viciously attacking both the ideas and character of his intellectual opponents, did something wonderful.

Something portraying infinite class.

Something portraying patience and poise.

Something portraying complete credibility.

He said, "yes, I am obviously not too fond of some of their ideas, but I still have tremendous respect for them."

Why is this so powerful?

Because it shows that you are not blinded by personal vendettas, which all-too-often lead people to try to undermine someone's ideas for no reason other than personal dislike.

And observers know that. It is so common, that they recognize your folly with ease.

People know that personal problems can turn someone against another's ideas, even if they would support those same ideas if they belonged to another person.

This strategy is brilliant because it shows that you are above the fray.

It shows that you are willing to say nice things about your opponents.

It shows that you are willing to unite in your commonalities, yet maintain respectful disagreements.

It shows that you are drastically, dramatically more objective and level-headed than most people in arguments are.

It shows that you are not fighting, but illuminating; not lengthening an argument, but working towards an agreement; not letting your personal problems drive your words, but using your words to dispel your personal problems.

All of these characteristics produce massive, immense, awe-inducing credibility.

And all you have to do to accomplish this is say extremely nice things about your intellectual opponents.

"I definitely see where you are coming from. I totally agree with [insert part of argument], and [insert part of argument]. That is the most eloquent defense of [insert position] I've ever heard, and it gives me a lot to think about. I respect your objectivity in this matter and appreciate the disagreement. My response is…"

That's all it takes.

It will instantly soften up your opponent.

It will instantly work magic for your credibility.

It will instantly turn any bystander in your favor.

It's simple, but effective.

Aesthetic Bias Part Two: How to Unlock the Hidden, Little-Known Language Patterns that Gives Ideas Influence and Words Power

Recall the aesthetic bias?

It is why people who say pretty words are more credible.

It is why well-spoken people are also well-believed people.

It is why virtually every single successful politician (a job which hinges more than most on creating public credibility) has the abundant ability to speak in aesthetically pleasing ways.

It is why eloquence is an inherently valuable, worthy end, in and of itself.

When we first discussed the aesthetic bias (about one hundred pages ago), I presented the rhetorical tools of rhetorical geniuses, dating back even to antiquity, but that are still used today.

Now, I'm going to uncover another element of the aesthetic bias: how to achieve it, and how to unlock proven language patterns that will instantly make your words more credible.

But first, let's talk about something else.

What is a quote?

Think about it.

Actually answer the question... what is a quote?

I'll tell you my answer as it relates to activating the aesthetic-impact bias to achieve tremendous credibility.

A quote is a set of words that are so eloquently arranged that they have been repeated by millions of people over thousands of years.

See where I'm going with this?

See how this connects to the aesthetic-impact bias?

If not, here's how: all you have to do to achieve the aesthetic-impact bias is to go grab a quote, break down its grammatical form, and fill that form in – that *formula* in – with your words.

Confused? You won't be after this example.

This is a fairly simple one.

Benjamin Franklin once said, "those things that hurt, instruct."

Think about the sentiment enclosed in this quote.

It's not particularly unique.

I've heard so many people say, "what hurts us usually has a lesson embedded in it that we can learn from," or "we should learn from our painful failures so that we don't repeat them."

This sentiment is not special.

This sentiment is common sense, common advice, and common knowledge.

So, what is special about Franklin's quote is not the sentiment encapsulated in it, but the way the words which convey that sentiment are arranged.

And here's what it all comes down to: to achieve the aesthetic-impact bias and gain credibility, you can adopt Franklin's formula.

"Those things that exceed expectations, produce profits."

"Those things that connect to customers, build brand equity."

"Those things that lower product quality, shorten firm longevity."

We're going to do a few of these.

Let's stick with the Franklin theme for some of them.

"Without freedom of thought, there can be no such thing as wisdom – and no such thing as public liberty without freedom of speech." That was Franklin.

"Without freedom of feedback, there can be no such thing as progress – and no such thing as a healthy culture without freedom of honest complaint."

"Well done is better than well said." That was Franklin.

"Well made is better than well marketed."

A brief side note: you must identify what parts of the quote give it its aesthetic impact, and not manipulate those in any way. For this one, the formula is "well [insert verb] is better than well [insert other verb]." You can't switch out the two wells, or the "is better than," because these elements are what create the aesthetic impact in the first place. That said, let's continue. Let's apply the three-step process of first choosing a quote, then identifying the elements we can safely switch out while preserving its aesthetic appeal, and then switching them out.

Step one: "Whatever is begun in anger ends in shame." Franklin.

Step two: "Whatever is begun in [insert quality] ends in [insert quality]."

Step three: "Whatever is begun in artificial short-term value-inflation ends in real long-term value-deflation."

Step one: "There was never a good war, or a bad peace."

Step two: "There was never a good [insert noun], or a bad [insert opposite noun]."

Step three: "There was never a good indifferent hire, or a bad ambitious one."

Step one: "Wealth is not his that has it, but his that enjoys it."

Step two: "[noun] is not his that has it, but his that [verb] it."

Step three: "Market share is not his that has it, but his that keeps it."

Step one: "He does not possess wealth; it possesses him."

Step two: "[noun] does not possess [noun]; it possesses [synonymous noun in different form, if needed]."

Step three: "Our business does not possess customers; customers possess our business."

Step one: "As we must account for every idle word, we must account for every idle silence."

Step two: "As we must [verb] for every [adjective] [noun], we must [identical verb] for every [identical adjective] [contrasting noun]."

Step three: "As we must reach for every untapped market, we must reach for every untapped ounce of efficiency potential." It's okay if your contrasting noun is a clump of nouns, as in this case.

Step one: "Hear reason, or she'll make you feel her."

Step two: "Hear [noun], or [pronoun and will conjunction] make you feel [pronoun]."

Step three: "Hear the customer complaints, or they'll make you feel them."

Step one: "A penny saved is a penny earned."

Step two: "A [noun] [saved synonym] is an [identical noun] [earned synonym]."

Step three: "A customer kept is a customer earned."

Step one: "Life's tragedy is that we get old too soon and wise too late."

Step two: "[noun in possessive form] tragedy is that we get [adjective] too soon and [adjective] too late."

Step three: "This firm's tragedy is that we get out of profitable positions too soon and into unprofitable ones too late."

Step one: "The first mistake in public business is the going into it."

Step two: "The first mistake in [insert activity] is the going into it."

Step three: "The first mistake in aggressive accounting is the going into it."

Alright, enough of Franklin.

Let's do some Obama, Reagan, and JFK, then move on from this altogether.

Step one: "My job is not to represent Washington to you, but to represent you to Washington." – Barack Obama.

Step two: "My job is not to represent [insert group] to you, but to represent you to [insert group]."

Step three: "My job is not to represent upper management to you, but to represent you to upper management."

Step one: "I don't oppose all wars. What I am opposed to is a dumb war. What I am opposed to is a rash war." – Barack Obama.

Step two: "I don't oppose all [plural noun]. What I am opposed to is a dumb [singular noun]. What I am opposed to is a rash [singular noun]."

Step three: "I don't oppose all stock buybacks. What I am opposed to is a dumb stock buyback. What I am opposed to is a rash stock buyback."

Step one: "Americans still believe in an America where anything's possible – they just don't think their leaders do." – Barack Obama.

Step two: "[plural noun] still believe in a [organization containing plural noun] where [aspirational noun] is possible – they just don't think their leaders do."

Step three: "Our employees still believe in a company where innovation is possible – they just don't think their leaders do."

Step one: "Trust, but verify." – Ronald Reagan.

Step two: "[verb or short action-oriented phrase], but [second verb or short action-oriented phrase qualifying the first]."

Step three: "Trade often, but hold more often."

Step one: "The future doesn't belong to the fainthearted; it belongs to the brave." – Ronald Reagan.

Step two: "The [noun] doesn't belong to the [adjective]; it belongs to the [opposing adjective]."

Step three: "The eCommerce industry doesn't belong to the profit-oriented; it belongs to the consumer-oriented."

Step one: "Government does not solve problems; it subsidizes them." – Ronald Reagan.

Step two: "[noun] does not solve problems, it [verb antonymous to solve] them."

Step three: "Optimistic accounting does not solve problems, it hides them."

Step one: "The greater our knowledge increases the more our ignorance unfolds." – JFK.

Step two: "The greater our [noun] increases the more our [contrasting noun] unfolds."

Step three: "The greater our customer service increases the more our profit potential unfolds."

Step one: "Those who make peaceful revolution impossible will make violent revolution inevitable." – JFK.

Step two: "Those who make [adjective] [noun] impossible will make [opposite verb] [identical noun] inevitable."

Step three: "Those who make a mediated solution impossible will make a court-mandated solution inevitable."

Step one: "Things do not happen. Things are made to happen." – JFK.

Step two: "[plural noun] do not happen. [identical plural noun] are made to happen."

Step three: "Exceeded projections do not happen. Exceeded projections are made to happen."

Inherency-Bias: How to Activate the Intrinsic-Quality Tendency with a Simple Kind of Magic Word that Creates Credible Communication

This one is interesting. It's yet another one of those psychological biases that can make your communication significantly more credible all by sprinkling around a few key words.

I'll tell you the key words, but first, let's talk about what this bias actually is.

Simply put: we find inherent qualities more credible than non-inherent qualities.

Confused? Don't worry. We'll break it down.

What is more credible, "aggressive accounting destroys the long-term financial health of the firm," or "aggressive accounting destroys the very goals it seeks to achieve, like the long-term financial health of the firm?"

The second one.

Why?

Because the second one exposes an inherent self-contradiction.

In other words, it exposes that the problems with aggressive accounting are a *part* of it, an *inescapable* feature of it, an inherent, intrinsic, fundamental component from which it cannot detach itself.

It exposes that problems with aggressive accounting are just... natural functions of aggressive accounting.

Why is it credible?

Because that which is inescapable, due to inherently being a part of something, is guaranteed. And that which is guaranteed is credible.

"Socialism is an evil ideology" is less compelling than "socialism is an inherently evil ideology," because the latter expresses that the ideology cannot escape the evil; that they are one and the same.

This is powerful.

And it's subtle.

But it comes down to this: speaking to the inherent, intrinsic, fundamental nature of something builds credibility because it is an absolute, leaving no room for ambiguity.

What do I mean by that?

To jump back to the socialism example, speaking to the inherent nature of it expresses that it is not evil because it produces evil outcomes, but because it, itself, in a vacuum, totally removed from the bad outcomes it produces, still has evil embedded at its core.

Things that are inherently good will always be good, and things that are inherently bad will always be bad.

Things that are good might produce bad outcomes in the context of externalities, and things that are bad might produce good outcomes in the context of externalities, but things that are inherently good will always produce good, because they themselves are the good, and the same holds true for things that are inherently bad.

Does that make sense?

It is the difference between "Socialism produces bad outcomes, therefore it is bad," and "Socialism is itself a bad outcome, by definition."

Even to me, this explanation is a little arcane and abstract, though the strategy that comes from it is very concrete.

So, what's the strategy?

Well, there are actually two strategies that both activate this bias. Let's get into them. Inherency-indicators activate the bias in your favor, making your statement more credible, whereas contradictory-nature statements make an alternative to your proposal less credible.

In other words, use inherency-indicators to gain credibility, and contradictory inherency-statements to reduce the credibility of an alternative to what you want, or to make your argument against something more credible by making that something less credible.

Use inherency-indicators. These simply state that your preferred alternative, proposal, decision, option, or solution is inherently, intrinsically, fundamentally, and by its very nature, good. So, what are inherency-indicators? Just like precision-bias activating words, and ease-bias activating words, and uniqueness-bias activating words, inherency-indicators are simply sprinkling around a set of key words and phrases that activate the bias. What are the key words for this bias? Well, I just said them: "inherently, intrinsically, fundamentally, by its very nature, by definition," are some of the most compelling, powerful, and easy to use. Think about it: what's more compelling, "the capital gains tax is fair because…" or "the capital gains tax is inherently, fundamentally fair because, by definition it is…?" I would say the second one.

Use contradictory inherency-indicators. These are simply saying that an alternative to your preferred option, or the opposing view, is inherently a bad thing. The "Socialism is an inherently evil ideology" example is a contradictory inherency-indicator. It is designed to bring the inherency bias to bear against something you don't like, whereas inherency-indicators bring it to bear in your favor.

Simple.

These words have impacts that go beyond what we tend to think.

In fact, most words do.

And that's a fundamental secret of rhetoric and credibility that many people miss.

But not us.

Jargon: How to Understand the Truth About Complex Trade- or Occupation-Specific Words, When to Use Them, and When to Not

This one is very interesting because most books on communication make one common mistake regarding jargon.

In fact, I confess: I made this same mistake myself in my first book. What's the mistake?

Explaining when Jargon is not a good idea and its detriments, but omitting when Jargon works, and how it can help build credibility in certain situations.

So, what is Jargon?

Jargon is trade-specific, occupation-specific, or expert language that most people outside of a group would not understand.

Market capitalization is Finance-Jargon.

Class-action appellate court jurisdictional purview is legal-Jargon.

Congressional institutional memory with regards to politico, trustee, and delegate representation is political-science-Jargon.

If you're speaking to financial experts, legal experts, or political science experts, go ahead and use your expert-level language.

The common piece of advice is this: stay away from Jargon because if your audience doesn't understand it, it can weaken trust, confuse them, and alienate them.

But what we often omit (not this time!) is this: if your audience actually understands the Jargon, then the truth is that it builds connection, personal ethos, and credibility, instead of destroying those things.

So, analyze your audience, and understand if they are experts on the subject you're speaking about.

Are they experts? Go ahead and use expert-level language, because they will see their expertise mirrored in you, feel a connection to you, and respect your knowledge and intellect (because it reminds them of their own).

Are they not experts? Stay away from Jargon.

A simple but important guideline that will prevent many embarrassing situations, but avoid preventing you from using this type of language in the right situations.

Wonderful.

Direct Authority Transfer: How to Borrow Credentials and Authority from the Most Compelling Source to Build Instant Credibility

Why do politicians appeal to party-identity?

Tribal appeals.

Team psychology appeals.

Intuitive-bias appeals.

Common enemy appeals.

Common symbology appeals.

Value appeals.

Belief-identification appeals.

Consistency appeals.

Doubt-avoidance appeals.

And hundreds of other reasons.

But the one we're going to talk about now is direct authority transfer.

Now, here's the foundation of this principle: when you are speaking, in most business situations, you are not only representing yourself but also the organization to which you belong.

And you almost always belong to some organization or group that has its own record or reputation, whether it is an entire company or a single department within one.

First, know this: authority comes from a positive record.

But what if you're new?

What if you don't have a record or reputation?

What if you can't point to anything in your history as evidence of your expertise and credibility?

Well, I have a solution for you, my friend.

It's called the direct authority-transfer principle.

What is it?

This: that you can directly borrow authority, reputation, and credibility from the organization you represent.

And that's why politicians so frequently perform party-appeals. That association can often boost their credibility (unless their audience is of the opposite party), because they borrow the authority and history of that party.

And what has more credibility?

What has a more impressive record?

What has a longer-standing reputation?

A new person with no record, or a party that has been around for over a century?

The same applies to a business.

What has more credibility?

The new salesman fresh out of college who, while appearing trustworthy and credible, has no real record to back him? Or, the corporation he represents, which has an extremely positive reputation, record, and 100-year-long history untainted by scandal?

Obviously, the corporation has more credibility.

But here's the best part: the salesman can experience direct authority-transfer, and draw upon the qualities of the organization he represents.

And this works both ways, positively and negatively, in one's favor and against it. It also works for multiple qualities, not just credibility.

Why do people automatically agree with politicians of their party, but also immediately despise politicians of the opposite party?

Because not only do the same-party politicians experience the direct transfer of positive qualities from the party they represent, like credibility, but those from the opposite party experience the direct transfer of negative qualities.

Snap categorization is part of the mechanism.

Remember that?

I'll leave it as an exercise for you to explain why snap categorization would function as a huge component of direct authority transfer.

So, how do we actually use direct authority transfer?

What do we say?

Although politicians have a reputation for being sneaky and untrustworthy, they get reelected in overwhelming numbers, and politicians not affiliated with a party (therefore having no authority to borrow) are scant to be seen.

Thus, we shouldn't hesitate to see how these people use direct authority-transfer.

And we should understand both the conscious, literal communication, and the sub-layer of subtextual, implicit, subconscious meaning.

We talked about unspoken words at the start, right?

Well, not only will we discover some ways politicians use authority-transfer, but we'll break down the unspoken words attached to each of these statements.

They'll say things like, "This is the party of progress, promise, and opportunity for everyone. This is the party that passed the Affordable Care Act, that is leading the push for a living minimum wage, that is responsible for every generous piece of legislation in the past three decades, like the earned income tax credit and the childcare tax credit. This party has a track record of fighting the good fight and winning, over, and over, and over again." The direct authority-transfer fueled subtext (which could not be spoken literally, and works only when implied) is this: "I am going to guarantee progress and opportunity for everyone, and though I have no record of doing so, the organization I have attached myself to does. While I have no record of passing any legislation, I am a part of a group that has pushed forward on medical care, the minimum wage, and wealth redistribution. Look at the record of the group I represent, and you will see the record I will build myself."

Or "This is the party which fought the civil war to end slavery and has been committed to protecting civil rights ever since. The difference between the two parties is that this one understands the wisdom of our constitution and how to protect it. Time and time again, we have succeeded in limiting greedy government overreach into your private lives and pocketbooks; time and time again, we have protected the American dream from implosion." The direct authority-transfer fueled subtext (which could not be spoken literally, and works only when implied) is this: "Look, I may not have been around to be given many opportunities to fight for civil rights, but the group I represent has, so you can bet that if an opportunity does arise, I'll be on the right side of history. I will fight for limited government, just like the group I represent has been doing for a long time. And that's the proof: you can see a history of civil liberty protection from my party, and that's what I will continue. It's why I'm a part of this party."

Or "This party is the most diverse it has ever been in its history, and much more so than the other party. Look at our most recent congressional cohort. We have a more representative group of people than has ever occupied Congress in this country's history, and we are the party that draws strength from diversity by accessing different viewpoints, stories, and cultures." The direct authority-transfer fueled subtext (which could not be spoken literally, and works only when implied) is this: "I am able to comprehend diverse perspectives and cultures, and cater to the unique problems of different demographics throughout this country, because as you can see, the party I represent is very diverse, though I may never have portrayed the ability to grasp diverse perspectives myself."

Does it seem silly when you're looking at the subtextual unspoken words?

Maybe they do seem silly.

But the human mind works in silly ways, performs silly shortcuts, and falls victim to silly oversights.

Recall snap categorization.

We see quality X in person Y (party affiliation), and snap categorize person Y to group Z (party members), thereby transferring onto the person the characteristics of group Z (like authority in fighting for a host of important political issues, for example). We do this even though the person does not necessarily have those characteristics.

How could a new software salesman discussing implementation, for example, adopt this strategy?

It's simple.

Instead of saying, "I have successfully helped clients implement this software, oh wait… that's right… zero times…? Okay, please accept my sincerest apologies… I'll head out for now…" they can say the significantly more credible "In the past year, we have successfully helped clients implement this software 2,500 times, with a 99% success rate."

Get it?

It's simple, straightforward, and easy, but insanely effective.

Superabundance: How to Unlock a Little-Known Element of Ancient Rhetoric That Defines Clear, Compelling, Credible Communication

Remember the first section on the aesthetic-impact bias?

Remember those rhetorical techniques, like anaphora, alliteration, and antithesis?

Well, those techniques are broadly organized under four core rhetorical principles that create compelling, credible communication.

And that's what we're talking about now.

So, let's get into superabundance.

Superabundance, in part, activates magnitude and fluency.

You'll see how.

Let's turn to two of the finest pieces of communication that ever came out of the United States: JFK's inaugural address and Martin Luther King's "I have a dream" speech.

More specifically, let's check out the two segments where superabundance is most evident.

JFK said, "Let every nation know, whether it wishes us well or ill, that we shall pay any price, bear any burden, meet any hardship, support any friend, oppose any foe, in order to assure the survival and the success of liberty."

MLK said, "This will be the day when all of God's children will be able to sing with a new meaning, "My country, 'tis of thee, sweet land of liberty, of thee I sing. Land where my fathers died, land of the pilgrim's pride, from every mountainside, let freedom ring." And if America is to be a great nation this must become true. So, let freedom ring from the prodigious hilltops of New Hampshire. Let freedom ring from the mighty mountains of New York. Let freedom ring from the heightening Alleghenies of Pennsylvania! Let freedom ring from the snowcapped Rockies of Colorado! Let freedom ring from the curvaceous slopes of California! But not only that; let freedom ring from Stone Mountain of Georgia! Let freedom ring from Lookout Mountain of Tennessee! Let freedom ring from every hill and molehill of Mississippi. From every mountainside, let freedom ring. And when this happens, when we allow freedom to ring, when we let it ring from every village and every hamlet, from every state and every city, we will be able to speed up that day when all of God's children, black men and white men, Jews and Gentiles, Protestants and Catholics, will be able to join hands and sing in the words of the old Negro spiritual, "Free at last! free at last! thank God Almighty, we are free at last!"

Now, you might be wondering why a book about credible business communication draws so much from political or civic speeches.

And the answer is that, more than any other pursuit, the political endeavor is, by its very nature, achieving credibility on a mass scale.

Not to mention that the famous political speeches have been recorded. So not only do they provide the best body of literature from which to draw credible communication principles, but they are easily accessible to all, whereas examples of effective business communication are not as great, but also not as accessible.

So, let's talk about superabundance.

It is also called addition, repetition, or expansion.

And that's truly all it is.

Just look: compare "Let every nation know that we shall *do anything* in order to assure the survival and the success of liberty," with "Let every nation know, *whether it wishes us well or ill, that we shall pay any price, bear any burden, meet any hardship, support any friend, oppose any foe,* in order to assure the survival and the success of liberty."

See what I mean?

See the power of superabundance?

See how JFK expanded "do anything" with that brilliant stream of promises? Of credible, confident commitments?

I'll let you observe the impact of superabundance in your own mind because that's where the impact of this (or any) communication strategy occurs.

Case in point: superabundance made JFK's statement (which was essentially that they would do anything) significantly, meaningfully, explosively more credible, because of the force behind it.

What about MLK?

The same principles apply.

Compare, "So, let freedom ring from *every single state*" to "So, let freedom ring from the prodigious hilltops of New Hampshire. Let freedom ring from the mighty mountains of New York. Let freedom ring from the heightening Alleghenies of Pennsylvania! Let freedom ring from the snowcapped Rockies of Colorado! Let freedom ring from the curvaceous slopes of California! But not only that; let freedom ring from Stone Mountain of Georgia! Let freedom ring from Lookout Mountain of Tennessee! Let freedom ring from every hill and molehill of Mississippi. From every mountainside, let freedom ring."

Compare "And when this happens, when we allow freedom to ring from *everywhere*…" to "And when this happens, when we allow freedom to ring, when we let it ring from every village and every hamlet, from every state and every city…"

Compare "We will be able to speed up the day when all of *God's children* will be able to join hands …" to "We will be able to speed up that day when all of God's children, black men and white men, Jews and Gentiles, Protestants and Catholics, will be able to join hands…"

See?

See the immense force of credibility created by the superabundance?

Mind you, this doesn't all occur consciously. These strategies have largely subconscious impacts. All that means is that they take impact in ways that influence the thought processes of the listeners outside of their awareness.

And that makes them yet more powerful.

But those speeches have a certain level of intensity that isn't appropriate for every business situation. I'm sure that's what you've been thinking.

And my answer: superabundance is not inherently intense and does not need to be to create credible communication.

Use superabundance of examples. In fact, all of these following types of superabundance use examples; you are breaking down a claim you make by providing a superabundance of support. "Countless financial institutions have fallen apart after aggressive accounting scandals – Enron, Krispy Kreme, WorldCom, [insert three to six more examples if needed]."

Use superabundance of options. In this case, the one clear, indisputable action emerges from the superabundance of options. The inundation, and the saturation of the superabundance, makes the singularity of the thing that must be done stand out from the rest. "We can do a lot; buy, hold, hedge, go for an option, short, but one thing is for sure, we must consult our expert on this industry before doing anything."

Use superabundance of risks. In this case, the superabundance serves to make something seem incredible; that is, un-credible, by providing a superabundance of risks. "This merger carries a lot of risks – lower stock valuation as a result of redundancies, employee turnover as their jobs are diluted, drastic dissatisfaction as core personnel are necessarily laid off, weakened brand image, management conflicts – so we must tread carefully. Every attempt to push this merger must be justified, not, as we've been acting, every attempt to resist it."

Use superabundance of negations. In this case, the superabundance of negations buries that which you negate under a mountain of overpowering counter-arguments. "This is not the wisest strategy – it is not responsible, it is not proven, it is not thought-out, it is not even with high-profit potential; it doesn't have the favor of our employees, our core management personnel are not happy about it, and there is no evidence that it will actually please our customers, but there is evidence that it will frustrate them."

Use superabundance of benefits. In this case, the superabundance of benefits is designed to support a proposal, decision, or option with an overwhelming weight of benefits. "I suggest this strategy because it is extremely beneficial – it will make us more efficient, it will reduce waste, it will raise profits and lower customer complaints, it will raise brand image and lower employee turnover, it will make us competitive for the next decade, and it will give us a massive advantage over our competitors."

Use superabundance of removed risks. In this case, the superabundance provides benefits not in the form of gains, but in the form of removed risks or prevented losses. This is also designed to provide an overwhelming weight of argumentative support. "This strategy will remove a tremendous amount of risk – the risk of litigation, the risk of competition from a startup, the risk of bad press as a result of the merger, the risk of lowered capitalization, the risk of reputational damage, and the risk of attracting the attention of activist investors."

Use superabundance of unknowns. In this case, the superabundance, much like the negation- or risk-based superabundance, is designed to lower the credibility of another alternative that you do not prefer. Negations are the most explicitly opposing kind, risk-based superabundance is more subtle, but the most subtle is the superabundance of unknowns. It simply casts doubt in the direction of an alternative because of the unanswered questions associated with it. "I would suggest caution. There are still a lot of unknowns associated with this approach – we don't know if it is cause for litigation, we don't know if there is competition from new startups, we don't know what our weaknesses in this new industry are, we don't know if the industry itself has a future in light of new technologies, we don't know if investors will see this as a positive move, we don't know if we have the personnel to staff this endeavor, we don't know if upper management is on board, we don't even know if the customers want this."

Use superabundance of actions. This is what JFK did. And this kind of superabundance, built around actions, inspires and motivates an audience. "We will do anything to remain competitive in this next decade – implement new programs, inspire new initiatives, observe new opportunities, innovate new products, build new branches, and expand across the globe."

Use superabundance with omitted platform. Superabundance launches off of a platform. For example, "we will do anything – [insert superabundance of actions], there are still a lot of unknowns associated with this approach – [insert superabundance of unknowns], this strategy will remove a tremendous amount of risk – [insert superabundance of risks], I suggest this strategy because it is extremely beneficial – [insert superabundance of benefits]." The platform, in a subtle and unintentional way, announces the theme of the items in the superabundance. But you can omit it. For example, JFK didn't say "Let every nation know, whether it wishes us well or ill, that we shall *do anything* – pay any price, bear any burden, meet any hardship, support any friend, oppose any foe, in order to assure the survival and the success of liberty." The omitted platform is more subtle, and is implicit communication, not explicit: instead of stating the platform and delineating the actions, the platform is implied by the actions. The superabundance does not come from the platform, but the platform is implied from the superabundance.

Use parallel superabundance. This strategy delivers the superabundance with a parallel structure. For example, JFK said, "…pay any price, bear any burden, meet any hardship, support any friend, oppose any foe." The structure "[verb] any [noun]," repeated five times. Every comma-delineated item shares the parallel structure in JFK's example.

Use alliterative superabundance. JFK also used alliterative superabundance (alliteration is inherently pleasing to the human mind, used in moderation): "…*p*ay any *p*rice, *b*ear any *b*urden"

Use anaphora-based superabundance. Anaphora repeats the key phrase over and over again (repetition is part of the essence of superabundance), and in doing so, roots the repeated phrase in the minds of the audience.

Anaphora is starting a sequence of subsequent clauses with a repeated phrase. For example, MLK repeated a series of clauses with "Let freedom ring…"

If you're wondering, the Latin word for superabundance is adiectio (I say, despite knowing that you probably weren't wondering).

Superabundance came from the ancient "rhetors:" masters of rhetoric.

It's no secret why their words have lived on for over two thousand years.

According to Wikipedia, the function of superabundance, or amplification, "refers to the act and means of extending thoughts or statements: to increase rhetorical effect, to add importance, to make the most of a thought or circumstance, to add an exaggeration, or to change the arrangement of words or clauses in a sequence to increase force."

What are the other three elements of ancient rhetoric?

Omission, or in Latin, *detractio*. It is also called subtraction, abridgement, or lack.

Omission is less important than superabundance.

Transposition, or in Latin, *transmutatio*. It is also called transferring.

Also, not as important.

And lastly, permutation, or *immutatio*, in Latin. It is also called switching, interchange, substitution, or transmutation.

Again, not as important.

For the purposes of credibility-building communication, superabundance is your friend. The others? They're more like polite, accidental acquaintances; you sort of like them when you run into them, but you don't seek them out.

The others are beyond the scope of this book, but not beyond the scope of one of my next books.

But there's a key principle here.

People have particular triggers.

Certain things will make them tick, while others will leave them completely cold.

For example, someone might be willing to jump onto a plan if and only if it has one specific benefit.

Great, right? They'll just ask, "Does this plan include [insert benefit]?"

Wrong.

They won't.

Why not?

Because they don't even know that benefit is what they are looking for; they don't even know that it's the specific key to their unique persuasive lock.

It's cliché but true: people don't always know what they want.

And even if they do, you probably won't always be able to find out.

You won't always be able to ask, "What are you looking for in a plan to do [insert goal]?"

So, how does this relate to superabundance?

In two ways.

For example, with the superabundance of benefits, the sheer mountain of benefits does two things.

Thing one: gradually builds desirability, heightening it with every single additional rapid-fire benefit. The same principle of intensifying a sentiment applies to all kinds of superabundance.

Thing two: increases your likelihood of hitting upon that specific magic benefit that is the key to getting the support of that particular person.

Get it?

The superabundance throws in a mountain of benefits, and thus increases your likelihood of hitting upon that one benefit that will count the most.

The Speed Guidelines: How to Apply a Simple, Easy, Little-Known Strategy to Make Your Talking Speed Build Your Credibility

If there's one theme that runs through every single strategy we've talked about so far, it is this: that human psychology works in certain ways, and effective communication plays upon those internal cognitive mechanisms.

And this one is no different.

So, what are the related psychological characteristics?

In other words, what are the mental input-output systems associated with the speed guidelines?

To clarify, input is what you do (or rather, what their senses perceive), and output is the thought in their head that results from those inputs.

So, here are the psychological characteristics.

There are four.

First, speaking fast makes you seem smart.

Sometimes.

Second, speaking fast makes you seem slick; a schemer, like a smooth-talking, fast-talking salesman.

Sometimes.

Third, speaking slowly makes you seem honest.

Sometimes.

Fourth, speaking slowly makes you seem a little dim-witted.

Sometimes.

So what do we have here?

Two speaking paces that each have a benefit and harm.

Two speaking paces that each have a pro and a con; a strength and a detriment.

Two speaking paces that reliably, based on the inherent features of human psychology, produce one of their associated harms or benefits.

I emphasize *sometimes* to emphasize the infinity of external variables that can cause a fast pace to appear smart versus slick, and vice-versa.

That said, how do you navigate these two paces and the impressions they produce?

Talk fast when you are rattling off your evidence, your support, your logic.

Talk fast when you are delivering impersonal stories, examples, statistics.

Talk fast when you are debunking opposing positions, arguing against something, or exposing logical flaws.

Seem smart.

Maybe even a little slick.

That's okay for now.

Then, when you are driving home the concluding point, the position you want your audience to personally adopt, the final, perhaps emotional persuasive punch, speak slow.

Seem honest.

Get it?

When you are listing off the benefits of your position, be fast.

When you are connecting your position to your audience, be slow.

When you are rattling off an impersonal story, be fast.

When you are explaining a personal and emotional story, be slow.

When you are delivering simple foundational logic, be fast.

When you are asking your audience to support you, be slow.

When you want to appear smart, talk fast, and when you want to appear honest, talk slow.

Not too fast, not too slow, but moderately fast and moderately slow.

Why do this?

Because who is more credible?

A smart but slick and sneaky person?

An honest but stupid one?

Or a smart and honest one?

By combining the two paces, you make yourself seem smart and honest, at the exact places when you need to be smart or honest, and unless you have any serious reputational or communication problems, you won't make yourself seem slick and stupid.

In other words, combining the paces is likely to tip you fully to the positive end of the two spectrums, not the negative ones, assuming that you're not doing anything else wrong in a major way.

Simple, but effective.

The P Quant Qual P Model: How to Combine the Two Types of Evidence to Instantly Appear Much More Credible with an Easy Structure

There are two types of evidence, and you need them both for maximum persuasion. As a refresher, here they are: quantitative evidence and qualitative evidence. The first kind can be regarded as logical, and the second as emotional. Quantitative evidence is made up of numbers. Quantitative evidence is made up of stories or examples. And the way they combine for persuasive power is like so: quantitative evidence appeals to the logical mind, and builds certainty; and the subsequent qualitative evidence appeals to the emotional mind, where influence actually occurs.

In other words: you need quantitative evidence, but only so that people's logical minds let their guard down, and you can punch straight at the emotional mind with an emotional qualitative example. Get it? If you go straight to the qualitative, you risk people thinking, "wait a minute… that's an anecdotal fallacy; you can't prove a rule with one anecdotal example." If you skip the qualitative and only use quantitative, you risk people thinking, "that's just a bunch of numbers… what do they even mean? How do I even interpret them?" And they will, on some level, think that: people are naturally horrible at dealing with statistics and much better at dealing with anecdotes and stories. But for the anecdotes and stories to take effect, you need to earn permission with the quantitative.

So, an adaptation of the PEP model is the P Quant Qual P model, and an analog to the PEEEEEBP example would be the P Quant Qual Quant Qual Quant Qual Quant Qual Quant Qual BP model. In other words: the stretching works for this too.

Here's an example. Point: "We need to solve income inequality." Quantitative evidence: "The top 1% made 50% of all new income in the past year." Qualitative evidence: "I spoke with a family in Iowa's fourth district; the father hasn't seen his kids in a week, since he works a night shift at his third job when they go to bed, and the mother had to drop out of school and give up her dreams to make ends, barely, just barely, meet." Point Repetition: "It's time to fix this now."

Get it? It's a simple model that you can use to instantly combine the two kinds of evidence in the best possible way.

Now, let's move on to another powerful strategy.

My favorite in this book.

And the final.

Advanced Reframing: How to Use a Highly Sophisticated, Little-Known Reframing Strategy for Easy Credibility and Fast Influence

Frames.

Frames are everything.

Frames are the key to controlling the minds of men and women.

Frames are the essence of advanced rhetoric.

Frames are a bit arcane, and I know that, despite all I have learned about them, there is still much more to discover.

Frames are a requirement for credible communication. By that, you must understand what they are, how to use them, and how to manipulate them in your favor.

Want to understand the basic essence of frames?

Observe this cartoon.

Worry not: our reframing techniques will not be as manipulative and dishonest as that cartoon.

But you'll see the similarities.

Go back and look at that cartoon after reading this chapter, and you'll see what it really means.

You'll also know that reframing techniques can be used for good.

Want to see Barack Obama use reframing in the 2012 presidential debate against Mitt Romney and make him look absolutely ridiculous?

Not that Obama is the only politician who does this.

Trump is incredibly adept at reframing.

But for now, let's use the Obama example.

Obama uses second-item-switching reframing.

So, what's a frame?

This: "X [insert relationship] Y."

What's second-item-switching reframing?

Turning "X [insert relationship] Y" into "X [insert relationship] Z." In other words, using an identical first item, an identical relationship, but a different second item.

In other words, it is the art of debunking an argument by expressing how the same argument applied to a different thing (the new item) results in an absurdity, thus making you seem extremely credible, and your opponent seem… not so credible.

And a quick note: an element of compelling reframing is the frame-presentation or frame-representation, in which you simply restate what your opponent said, before building a new frame. You simply present their frame before changing it in your favor. This makes your reframing more compelling by clearly portraying the contrast between your opponent's frame and your new frame, which, if you do this correctly, is something you absolutely want.

In other words, you want your opponent's frame to be fresh in mind when you reframe.

And if there's no opponent? Well, we'll talk about that later.

You'll see how Obama does this.

Let's see the transcripts.

"Romney: Our Navy is old – excuse me, our Navy is smaller now than at any time since 1917. The Navy said they needed 313 ships to carry out their mission. We're now at under 285. We're headed down to the low 200s if we go through a sequestration. *[Frame one set by Romney: X = our navy, the relationship = has, and Y = less ships than 1917… "Our navy has less ships than in 1917].* That's unacceptable to me. I want to make sure that we have the ships that are required by our Navy. Our Air Force is older and smaller than at any time since it was founded in 1947. We've changed for the first time since FDR – since FDR we had the – we've always had the strategy of saying we could fight in two conflicts at once. Now we're changing to one conflict. Look, this, in my view, is the highest responsibility of the President of the United States, which is to maintain the safety of the American people. And I will not cut our military budget by a trillion dollars, which is a combination of the budget cuts the president has, as well as the sequestration cuts. That, in my view, is making – is making our future less certain and less secure.

Obama: Bob, I just need to comment on this. First of all, the sequester is not something that I've proposed. It is something that Congress has proposed. It will not happen. The budget that we are talking about is not reducing our military spending. It is maintaining it. But I think Governor Romney maybe hasn't spent enough time looking at how our military works. You mentioned the Navy, for example, and that we have fewer ships than we did in 1916. *[Obama performs frame-representation, repeating what Romney said to him; reiterating frame one so that it is fresh in the minds of the audience and the reframing doesn't fall flat. He says, in essence, "You mentioned (insert frame one, which Romney set)].* Well, Governor, we also have fewer horses and bayonets, because the nature of our military's changed. *[This line is said to have ended that debate for Romney and to have been one of the most brilliant lines in all of political debating. It's insanely simple if you break down the reframing technique. Frame one was set by Romney: "We (X) have (relationship) less ships than in 1917 (Y)." Frame two, set by Obama, reframed frame one with second-item-switching; it retained the X and the relationship, but applied Z instead of Y as the second item: "We (X) have (relationship) fewer horses and bayonets (Z)," where Z is an item that results in an absurdity when Romney's logic is applied to it].* We have these things called aircraft carriers, where planes land on them. We have these ships that go underwater, nuclear submarines."

Do you see?

Frame one: "We have less ships than in 1917."

Frame two: "We also have less horses and bayonets."

Get it?

Second-item-switch reframing is often signaled by the word "also," for example, "we *also* have less horses and bayonets." This word signals the application of frame-one logic to a new second item (the Z which replaced the Y) and primes us to see the symmetry between the logic, making it more impactful when we see that it leads us to an absurdity.

Frames can have a fourth and fifth component, though this is second-tier framing, in which they take, for example, this form: "X (1) [insert relationship] (2) Y (3), because (4) [reasons] (5)," (for example, "We have less ships than in 1917 because Obama sequestered some ships), or "X (1) [insert relationship] (2) Y (3), [insert equivalency] Z," (for example, "We have less ships than in 1917, which is bad).

We're dealing with first-tier reframing.

But as a quick aside, Obama's second-tier frame was, "We also have less horses and bayonets because the nature of our military has changed." (X [insert relationship] Y because [insert reasons]).

All of the reframing techniques we are working with today are tier one, and as you can see, are accessible in all situations. Just because Obama had a "because" doesn't make the initial reframing any less powerful. Tier one frames are contained in tier two frames.

So, ignore tier-two reframing for now.

Again, there are particular kinds of reframing strategies that are extremely compelling.

I know of *some*.

I promise you that there are many, many more I have yet to discover. But when I do, you'll be the first to know.

So, what are some critical types of reframing?

What are some reframing strategies that instantly make you seem sharp as a tack, extremely well-researched, and highly credible (while making anyone who argues against you seem… not those things)?

Let's get into it.

Use reversal-reframing. Reversal framing is maintaining all three items in the first frame but changing their order. Instead of "X [insert relationship Y]," "identical Y [insert identical relationship] identical X." This is particularly useful for causation-related arguments when you want to explain how your opponent has the cause and the effect mixed up. For example, let's say you're arguing that campaign funds are not important in achieving election. Let's say your opponent says "Campaign funds (X) cause (relationship) political success (Y), because [reasons]..." you can say "Political success (identical Y in X's former position) causes (insert identical relationship) campaign funds (identical X in Y's former position) because the candidate who is most popular and most likely to win an election is also most likely to get the most funds. *[Why not throw in a quick sententia summation to activate the intuitive bias?]* Funds don't cause popularity; popularity causes funds. *[See how all of these strategies work together, and how this book is, from beginning to end, a complete, consistent, credibility-continuum? See how you can draw a strategy from one of the first chapters, to activate one of the first psychological tendencies, and apply it to this strategy?]* In summary, frame one = "Funds cause political success," frame two = "Political success causes funds."

Use escalation-reframing. Escalation reframing is maintaining the frame-one X, the frame-one relationship, but expanding Y to a less specific version of itself. "X [insert relationship] Y" becomes "X [insert relationship] a less specific Y." This is a good strategy if the details are not in your favor. For example, in the 2016 Republican primary, Marco Rubio's frame one was "Trump (X) hired (relationship) illegal immigrants (Y)." Trump performed frame escalation by presenting his frame, frame two, which escalated on frame one by saying "I (X – identical to "Trump" when Trump is speaking), am the only one up here who hired (specified relationship) people (escalated Y)." This emphasized his successful business background. The category "people" contains the category "illegal immigrants." It is just tracing the category-chain to an unspecific, broader category, which works in Trump's favor. Note that escalating, broadening, and expanding the Y (from illegal immigrants to people) necessitates specifying the relationship (from "hired" to "am the only one who hired.") Rubio's frame one had X (Trump), an unspecific relationship (hired) and a specific Y (illegal immigrants), while Trump wanted to distract the attention from his having hired illegal immigrants (which was not politically popular in his party), so he said X (I – Trump) a specific relationship (am the only one up here who hired) and an unspecific Y (people). This draws attention away from his hiring of illegal immigrants, and towards the fact that he has managed a large organization for a long time, and is an American businessman, which is politically popular within his party. Note that the two frames are not a battle of facts, but a battle that seeks to answer this question: "at which level of specificity will we have this argument?" The two frames have no fact-based disagreement with one another. In summary, frame one = "Trump hired illegal immigrants," frame two = "I'm the only one up here who has hired anybody."

Use specification-reframing. Escalation reframing is maintaining the frame-one X, the frame-one relationship, but expanding Y to a less specific version of Y, which often necessitates a more specific frame-one relationship. Specification reframing is the opposite. When the core facts are in your favor, and you want to hone in on them, specification is your friend. It is reframing a frame one of "X [insert relationship] Y" to "identical X [insert identical relationship] more specific Y." Rubio, in the last example, spoke first, so he did not reframe; he just framed. And the most recent frame gets the attention. If Trump had started by saying "I (X) am the only one up here who has hired (relationship) people (Y)," then Rubio would have had the opportunity to reframe by frame-specification, and say "You (identical X) hired (similar relationship) illegal immigrants (more specific Y)." If the facts are in your favor, specify. If the facts are not, escalate to a level of specificity where they are. In summary, frame one = "I'm the only one up here who's has hired anybody," frame two = "You've hired illegal immigrants."

Use relationship-changing reframing. This type of reframing maintains the X, the Y, but changes the relationship between them. "X [insert relationship] Y" becomes "identical X [insert new relationship] identical Y." For example, "The capital gains tax (X) reduces (relationship) investment activity (Y)" is reframed to "The capital gains tax (identical X) doesn't impact (new relationship) investment activity (identical Y)." Now, to be truthful, and as you can possibly see from the example, this is one of the less compelling reframing models. However, there's a specific type of relationship-changing reframing that is extremely compelling. It's up next. In summary, frame one = "The capital gains tax reduces investment activity," frame two = "The capital gains tax doesn't impact investment activity."

Use relationship-reversal reframing. Relationship-changing reframing is simply changing the relationship between the X and the Y. Relationship-reversal reframing is completely reversing the relationship; it is maintaining the X and the Y, and not only changing the relationship but reversing it to its opposite. The basic form is reframing "X [insert relationship] Y" to "X [insert completely opposite relationship] Y." For example, turning "X supports Y" to "X contradicts Y." "Supports" and "contradicts" are opposites. Get it? For example, "The capital gains tax reduces investment activity" is reframed to "The capital gains tax increases investment activity." It is saying, without actually saying, "not only are you wrong, but you are the most possible amount of wrong." Now, we'll get into this later, but the "X [insert relationship] Y" formula is often abstract, and implicitly stated, because the grammar of an actual statement is different. For example, I once heard someone say, "People ask me how I can be both [insert political position one] and [insert seemingly contradictory political position two] at the same time. My answer is that it is because I am [insert political position one] that I am [insert seemingly contradictory political position two]." This implicitly has the relationship-reversal form, though it is not presented in the straightforward formula we use to understand this reframing model. In summary, drawing from that indirect example of relationship-reversal reframing, frame one = "This political position I hold contradicts this other political position I hold," frame two = "This political position I hold is the reason I hold this other political position."

Use second-item-switching. This was the Obama example. "X [insert relationship] Y" becomes "identical X [insert identical relationship] Z," where Z makes evident that the logic results in an absurdity. To do this successfully, do what Obama did: precede it with frame-representation, deliver it with using as many identical words to frame one as you can, use "also" to signal the logical symmetry, and make your statement grammatically parallel to the first frame. In summary, frame one = "We have less ships than in 1917," frame two = "We also have less horses and bayonets."

Use first-item-switching. This is useful if a quality is applied to something, and you want to change the thing to which it is applied. The form is "X [insert relationship] Y" to "Z [insert identical relationship] identical Y." "The capital gains tax reduces investment" becomes "A weak social safety net and degrading amount of social capital, which the capital gains tax is used to fix, reduces investment." This can take on the qualities of escalation if the new X – the Z – seems to build upon the initial X by broadening the perspective, including more detail, expanding the body of evidence upon which the judgment is formed, or broadening out to include a more complex web of second and third-order consequences. This is exactly what we did with this example: the capital gains tax may or may not reduce investment, but an intact social safety net, competent regulatory environment, and abundance of social capital definitely do increase investment in a big way, and those are the things the capital gains tax pays for. In summary, frame one = "The capital gains tax reduces investment," and frame two = "A weak social safety net and degrading amount of social capital reduces investment." This is most effective if the relationship between the frame one X (the capital gains tax) and the frame two Z, which replaced the X (in this case, a weak social safety net and degrading amount of social capital) is widely understood. In this case, the reframing is most compelling if the audience widely understands that the X (the tax) is used to pay for the Z. If it is not, then enumerate the relationship between the X and the Z: "A weak social safety net and degrading amount of social capital, *which the capital gains tax is used to fix*, reduces investment."

Use no-opponent frame-presentation. What if you have no opponent, thus no frame one to reframe into a frame two? Well, this strategy is your friend. Let me show you. All you have to do is say, "there are some who say [insert frame one]." For example, in a conference devoted to progress on global issues faced by women, Hillary Clinton said that "There are some who question the reason for this conference. *[This past sentence is frame presentation of another frame held by a vaguely defined but still relevant group.]* Let them listen to the voices of women in their homes, neighborhoods, and workplaces. *[This past sentence is frame escalation. She now has a frame to escalate off of and challenge because she presented it in the previous sentence.]* There are some who wonder whether the lives of women and girls matter to economic and political progress around the globe. *[She expands on her previous frame presentation by exposing another facet of the opposing frame she is presenting and responding to.]* Let them look at the women gathered here and at Huairou – the homemakers and nurses, the teachers and lawyers, the policymakers and women who run their own businesses. *[Once again, after presenting another aspect of an opposing frame, Hillary escalates off of it.]* It is conferences like this that compel governments and peoples everywhere to listen, look, and face the world's most pressing problems. Wasn't it after all – after the women's conference in Nairobi ten years ago that the world focused for the first time on the crisis of domestic violence?"

Use tier-two reframing. Surprise! It's back. I just wanted to take a quick moment to remind you how all of these reframing models we just covered are contained in tier two frames. They all benefit from a "because [reasons]," to justify the tier-one frame, or "which is [insert third item]," to explicitly and clearly elaborate on the significance of the tier-one frame. For example, reframing "X proves Y" to "X contradicts Y" would obviously benefit from adding "because [reasons]" to the new frame. Tier-two reframing simply supplements tier-one reframing.

Use frame-formula-reduction. I've alluded to this before. I'll address it now. People do not always phrase things in the neat, orderly frame formula of "X [insert relationship] Y." But nearly every single statement one might make is synonymous with a statement made in that frame formula. So, figure out the implicit frame formula that they are presenting, by cutting away at the unnecessary, defining their position in the most basic, simple, and reduced way, and then altering that to fit the frame formula. You are not changing their meaning, just presentation. Why? To put it in a way that is more useful for you; to put it in a way that you can more readily reframe from.

Use frame-formula-reduction frame presentation. In a debate, discussion or argument, reframing is most effective if you re-present the opposing frame to refresh people's memory of it, and then present your new frame with grammatically parallel language. So, perform frame-formula reduction (pulling out the basic frame proposed in a complex web of words), and then re-present this reduced frame formula, so that your reframing is yet more compelling. This brings all the statements down to their core essentials; their fundamental basics. And this is what makes your reframing yet more compelling. It makes it as neat, snappy, and clear as "We have less ships than in 1917... We also have less horses and bayonets." Make sure you are not committing the strawman fallacy. What's that? Responding to an argument that your opponent did not actually make. Misunderstanding their position and responding to this misunderstanding instead of what they actually said. Make sure that when you perform frame-formula-reduction, you are not altering the meaning of the frame. Ask yourself this: would this person ever say, "no, that's not what I meant..." when you say "what you're saying is [insert frame-formula-reduction frame presentation]?" To repeat: a frame-formula-reduction frame presentation is first, accurately rephrasing your opponent's position in the frame formula, presenting this (for example, "you mentioned that [insert frame]"), and then reframing off of it. And to repeat again: you do this because it makes the reframe more compelling and clearer when you deal with frames in their simplified, parallel nature. The key consideration is this: from every web of words, you can pull out a set of statements (one or more) that are phrased in the simple frame formula. Even if they didn't phrase it that way, whatever they did say will be synonymous with some set of words in the simple frame formula. It's easier than it sounds. Just ask yourself, "what is this person saying, if I had to summarize it as a first thing, a relationship, and a second thing?"

Use proof-burden reframing. After you've done *something* to prove your point, you can use this to shift the proof-burden onto the other people. It's tricky, sneaky, and slick. But fun. Let me explain. The burden of proof – that is, the responsibility to prove a claim – lies squarely with the person making it. Logically, at least. You can't say, "you can't disprove my claim; therefore, it's true!" It's on you to prove your claim, not on the people who disagree with you to disprove it. Just because they can't disprove it doesn't mean it's proven; the burden of proof still sits at your feet, waiting to be satisfied. But remember what a logical fallacy signals: that human beings tend to make a repetitious thinking mistake. That's what the fallacy is: the repetitive thinking mistake. So, I'm not saying to ever, *ever* do this without providing some proof of your position, but once you do, you can subtly perform the fallacy by shifting the burden of proof to your audience (and it won't really be a fallacy since you already provided proof – it will just be persuasive icing on the cake). For example, when you are arguing in favor of a certain cause and effect relationship, provide proof, and then ask the question "why else would it happen?" This shifts the burden of proof from you to your audience. This shifts the situation from "I'm going to prove to you why this is the reason that thing is happening," to "You prove to me that there's even another reason that could cause it." The vast majority of the time, they will not be able to respond to this with a fluent magnitude of explanation or evidence. Remember: this is only ever appropriate after providing genuine proof. Prove your point, then prompt the others to prove an alternative to your point; in the absence of any alternatives or people who can eloquently express them, this will make your point seem more proven. A variation of this is "why else would [insert person] do [insert action], if not [insert your explanation]?" Remember, people love to see the world through a lens of cause and effect. They want to find an explanation for everything. This strategy makes your explanation the only explanation. This is a type of meta-reframing or situational-reframing. But that's a story for another day.

My Final Words

Thank you for trusting me and reading this book.

Thank you for giving me the cherished gift of communicating these ideas to you.

Thank you for making it possible for me to write about the subject I love for a living.

I hope we have connected through these pages. And I am filled with gratitude, because to me, we have.

I hope these pages served you and helped you accomplish one of the most worthwhile goals: becoming a better communicator.

I hope you trust me when I tell you that there is no final destination; there is no stopping point, only constant improvement. You must practice this critical skill of communication every single day, in every single way, because it is a gift to mankind.

We have a special, sacred, unique gift – the gift of spoken word, of connection through airwaves – and we must use it; must not let it rust away and whither, but exercise it day in and day out.

Through this gift, we can stop or start any mass movement that ripples throughout history long after we leave this Earth.

Through this gift, we can chart a course for our lives and follow it with renewed vigor and greater potential.

Through this gift, we can make the most of this life we've been given and help others do the same.

Through this gift, we can inundate the minds of our fellow humans with ideas that are bold, brave, valuable, and viciously worthwhile; we can break through the barrier that stands between what we want and what we have, by forming big, brave coalitions of the convinced.

It is not a question of *if* you will speak, or even of *when*, but of *how*.

Will you wield a polished, poised, and precise tool, or one that is dead, degraded, and dulled from the disgrace of disuse?

Will your words be believed, or tossed aside?

Alive with potential, or dead on arrival?

Heeded, or ignored?

Credible, or incredible?

If I've accomplished my goal, you didn't have to think about those questions before you knew the answer.

Thank you for letting me try. I hope I've succeeded, just as I hope that you will.

Sincerely, Peter – your partner in striving for success, for the love of the journey, not the destination.

Bonus Chapter #1: How to Reliably Build the Best Mindset for Confident Communication (From How to Master Public Speaking)

"This is, beyond the shadow of a single doubt, the most important section of this book. And this, beyond the shadow of a single doubt, is the most important word: *confidence*.

Confidence is what will push you towards success as a speaker, or hold you back from it. You have to truly believe in your ability to be an amazing speaker. Believe in it, and the hard work will become much easier because you will see the desired outcome as *genuinely attainable*. See yourself as an unstoppable speaker, and you will become one. Keep this thought in the back of your mind - that you are a good public speaker - every time you speak publicly. Find your own variation of that thought. Some people prefer "I'm an unstoppable public speaker," while others prefer the humbler, "I'm a solid public speaker who can give a good presentation to these wonderful people gathered here today."

Don't be afraid to get out of your comfort zone. Your ability to be an effective public speaker is split not only into *what* you say but *how* you say it. Be confident in yourself to maximize the power of the "how you say it." The first stepping stone to completely uninhibited speech is confidence in oneself. Master confidence and all else in public speaking will come much more easily.

Understandably, it's not quite as easy as saying, "I'm going to be confident now." The secret in developing public speaking confidence lies in facing anxiety, time and time again until it disappears and you've conquered it once and for all. Being at that point is incredibly tranquil, and it is here where the confidence gained from public speaking finally spills into other areas of life. Audiences can hear confidence. They can see it, and they can notice when it's missing.

Developing public speaking confidence doesn't come easy, but once it does, everything else will fall into place."

You can purchase *How to Master Public Speaking* from this link: <u>http://bit.ly/public-speaking-book</u>

Bonus Chapter #2: How to Persuade with Easy, Proven Strategy (From Effective Communication: The Patterns of Easy Influence)

Use the path contrast structure. What it is: structuring your speech by contrasting two different possible paths. Contrasting a "good" proposed path and a "bad" alternative.

Why it works: It frames the contrast between the two paths, which allows you to control the narrative. It uses contrast persuasion, one of the most effective persuasive methods. It lets you make your proposed path seem like the obvious choice.

When to use it: when you want to persuade, motivate, or inspire your audience to take one path instead of another when there is uncertainty about how to proceed. When the future is unclear, and you want to lead the way.

The step-by-step process. Good path: "Here's the good path we should take." Good outcome: "Here are the good things that will happen if we do." Alternative path: "Or, here's a bad alternative path we could take." Alternative outcome: "And here are the bad outcomes that will happen if we do." Back-and-forth: Jump back and forth between describing the good path and the alternative path.

Let me tell you a secret: persuasion is more powerful when it has contrast. (I call it "contrast persuasion"). In other words: if you want people to take a path, don't only talk about the benefits of that path. Contrast the "good" path with an alternative "bad" path.

So, don't only say this: "Imagine our lives when we take [good path]. We will [insert benefit 1], [insert benefit 2], and [insert benefit 3]."

You must also say this: "Imagine our lives when we take [bad path]. We will [insert consequence 1], [insert consequence 2], and [insert consequence 3]."

And then jump back and forth between them. Hit the contrast button over and over again. Make it a glaring, obvious, clear answer that they should take the good path. How? By repeatedly and vividly contrasting it with a bad one.

Why is this such a powerful strategy? The contrast between the "good" and "bad" outcome is more persuasive than either of them alone. Presenting a "good" option that you want, and a "bad" alternative, makes doing what you want the obvious action. I repeat: making it seem like a contrast between two options allows you to control the narrative. Another persuasive speech structure that uses contrast persuasion is up next.

Use the past-present-means structure. What it is: presenting the problems of your difficult past, shifting to the easy, successful present, and explaining how you made the transition.

Why it works: it builds audience relatability by resonating emotionally. It shows the contrast between having unsolved problems and solved problems. It makes the "means" extremely desirable.

When to use it: When you want to influence or persuade your audience to do something (whatever your "means" are). When your proposed action worked personally for you in your life. When your life before taking the proposed action matches the lives of your audience now.

The step-by-step process: Past: "Here's how my life was difficult in the past. Here were my unsolved problems. I was suffering in the ways you are suffering." Present: "Here's how my life is successful now. Here's what it's like to have the problems solved. Here's how I'm no longer suffering, and life is easy." Means: "Here's the exact solution I personally used to get from the difficult past to the successful present."

This speech structure is so damn powerful. The entire time you're in the past and present stages, your audience is going *crazy*... wondering: "How did you do it? How did you solve the problem? Help me! Can you please show me the solution? I need this in my life! I want to do what you did!"

And then bam: you hit them with that solution. And at this point, there's almost nothing that can stop them from taking it (whether it's something they buy or something they simply do).

The curiosity, suspense, and intrigue built up during the two phases of your personal story (past and present) are too strong.

Here are the crucial principles. Humility: yes, you solved the problem they are struggling with. Yes, you still have to be humble about it. Honesty: don't you dare make your past and present seem like anything other than what they are. Relatability: is your past really similar to the current lives of your audience members? Emotional resonance: can you accurately depict the emotions you felt during the difficult past? Can you convey them to your audience? If you do, will they think, "wow, that's exactly how I feel right now?"

And some important guidelines: don't present the solution until step three. In other words: don't let step two and three blend. In step two, only explain the relief from the problem. Don't explain how it happened. This builds curiosity and suspense. Show vulnerability in step one: be open, honest, and willing to expose parts of your past. In step three, describe the solution at length. Emphasize how it worked for you. Imply that if it worked for you, it can work for them.

Use the problem-solution structure. What it is: presenting a clear problem your audience has, and then presenting a solution to that problem.

Why it works: it ensures that your audience understands why your solution matters. It educates your audience and provides value. It points out a problem which your audience might not have known about.

When to use it: when you want to persuade your audience to solve a problem. When they might not be aware of the problem, or how serious it is. When you are selling a solution.

The step-by-step process: Problem presentation: "Here's a problem you didn't know you had." Problem consequences: "Here's why this problem is worse than you think." Solution presentation: "But there's a solution." Solution outcome: "Here's what it will feel like when you solve the problem."

This persuasive speech structure is so simple. But so powerful. Here's why: most people make the mistake of only talking about their solution, which is *bad*, because a solution only makes sense in the context of a problem. In other words: why do so many people talk about their solutions without first explaining the problem it solves? Because they haven't read this book. But you have :) Time for number six: a structure very similar to this one.

You can purchase *Effective Communication: The Patterns of Easy Influence* **from this link: bit.ly/effective-comm-book**

Bonus Chapter #3: How to Sentiment-Map (From Interpersonal Communication: How to Win Clients and Influence Teams)

This one is simple. But powerful. Here it is: sentiment = pw - nw, where pw = positive words, and nw = negative words. Get it? Essentially, this equation determines if the sentiment of your speech is positive or negative. And you can apply *any* qualities instead of positive or negative, and give it a shot. The problem is that not many dualities are as broad, descriptive, and useful as positive and negative.

Let's break down this equation. If you say 100 words, and 20 of them are positive, and 10 are negative, your sentiment equation yields the number 10. 20 positive words minus 10 negative words. Thus, you have mathematically determined that your communication is positive. But what if you want it to be more positive? This equation is your friend. Add more positive words, or remove the 10 negative words, or replace the 10 negative words with 10 positive words, or all three. In other words: this equation will instantly help you determine if the overall sentiment if your speech is positive or negative, and it will help you adjust accordingly.

We'll get to an example in a moment. But first, we have to talk about why it's so important to understand this equation. And here's why: clumps of positive words produce certain emotional reactions; clumps of negative words produce certain different emotional reactions; and depending on your communication goals, you want one of those reactions. And in some cases, you want a clump of one sentiment, followed by a clump of the other. But what you never want is this: a sentiment score of 0, unless it is produced by a concentrated, punchy clump of one sentiment, followed by its opposite, which numerically cancel out.

In other words: [pw] [pw] [pw] [pw] [pw] [pw] [nw] [nw] [nw] [nw] [nw] [nw], is good; why? Because the two clumps produce two distinct, potent emotional reactions that are strengthened by their contrast, even though the sentiment score is 0, or neutral. This is the limitation of this equation. Is it really neutral? Is an extreme positive emotional reaction followed by an extreme negative reaction neutral? Mathematically, they cancel out, but in reality, they do not undo each other like that. So, while that example is strong, [pw] [nw] [pw] [nw] [pw] [nw] [pw] [nw] [pw] [nw] [pw] [nw] is not. Why? Because the two opposite sentiments are diffused amongst one another and intertwined in such a way that there is no distinct, unambiguous, unequivocal sentiment at any point.

What reactions do positive sentiments produce? Well, *positive reactions*: elation, elevation, hope, happiness, faith, strength, optimism, and the like.

And negative? Anger, loss, discomfort, discontent, unhappiness, and the like. So, here's the rule: identify which type of emotional reaction is most likely to bring your audience to the action you want them to take, and use the sentiment equation to gear your words in that direction.

And here's the second rule: if you are speaking for action, avoid a sentiment score of 0 produced by scattered words of opposite sentiment. There will be no compelling emotional reaction. (Well there might be, depending on whatever else you are doing and saying. I should say there will be no compelling emotional reaction as a result of your semantic sentiment).

While a sentiment score of 0 produced by scattered words of opposite sentiment produces no coherent and compelling reaction, a sentiment score of 0 produced by a section with a sentiment score of positive 50 followed by a sentiment score of negative 50 will produce not zero emotional reactions, not one emotional reaction, but two; a positive one, followed by a negative one.

And there is a specific strategy that takes advantage of this mode of sentiment mapping. As a brief preview, here's what you do: contrast a proposed good path (your idea) with an alternative. First, describe the alternative, then describe your proposed path. Use very high negative sentiment when describing the alternative, and very high positive sentiment describing your proposed path. Get it? The audience will associate the alternative to your idea with negativity, and your idea with positivity. Sure, the sentiment score will be 0 overall, but only because there is first a very high negative sentiment score, and a very high positive sentiment score. And this is not at all neutral. The sentiment score equation is limited by this feature.

However, we can overcome this limitation if we localize the sentiment score, applying it to specific sections of a communication, instead of the whole. For example: [pw] [pw] [pw] [pw] [pw] [pw] (sentiment score = 6; high positive sentiment score = strong positive emotional reaction) [nw] [nw] [nw] [nw] [nw] [nw] (sentiment score of this section = -6; high negative sentiment score = strong negative emotional reaction).

On the other hand, no matter how you divide up [pw] [nw] [pw] [nw] [pw] [nw] [pw] [nw] [pw] [nw] [pw] [nw], you will always have a sentiment score of 0 or near 0, meaning that at any point in your speech, your semantic sentiment is producing no particular emotional reaction (although other things might be). This is a lost opportunity.

Before moving on to our third and final equation, let us examine an example of the sentiment score at play, taken from Donald Trump's 2019 State of the Union address:

"As we have seen, when we are united [+1], we can make astonishing [+1] strides [+1] for our country [+1]. Now, Republicans and Democrats must join [+1] forces again to confront [+1] an urgent [-1] national crisis [-1]. The Congress has 10 days left to pass a bill that will fund [+1] our Government, protect [+1] our homeland [+1], and secure [+1] our southern border. Now is the time for the Congress to show the world that America is committed [+1] to *[dividing line]* ending illegal [-1] immigration and putting the ruthless [-1] coyotes [-1], cartels [-1], drug dealers [-1], and human traffickers [-1] out of business. As we speak, large, organized caravans [-1] are on the march [-1] to the United States. We have just heard that Mexican cities, in order [-1] to remove the illegal [-1] immigrants from their communities [+1], are getting trucks and buses to bring them up to our country in areas where there is little border protection. I have ordered another 3,750 troops [-1] to our southern border to prepare [+1] for the tremendous [-1] onslaught [-1]."

Let's check out the alternating sentiments: "+ + + + + + - - + + + + + [dividing line] - - - - - - - - - + - + - -"

Let's check out the overall sentiment rating: 13 positive words minus 14 negative words = -1. This is negligible, and based on the length of the communication, a +3 or -3 range around zero can be regarded as 0.

But remember the limitation of sentiment score, and identify the localized scores on each side of the dividing line (which can be found at the point in communication when a sequence that is extremely positive or negative ends, and is replaced by an opposing sequence). "+ + + + + + - - + + + + +" = 11 positive words minus 2 negative words, with an extremely high positive sentiment score of 9. And across the dividing line, "- - - - - - - - - + - + - -" = 2 positive words minus 12 negative words, with an extremely high negative sentiment score of -10. See the power of localized sentiment? And before we get into why Trump used this alternating sentiment strategy, we have to cover one last point.

Context is that last point. I'll keep this brief so we can get into the further analysis a little quicker. You'll see that context determines the positive or negative sentiment of certain words. In the first section, "country" is +1. In the second, it is -1.

How can one word have two different sentiment values? Because of where they are, and their context: in the first half, it was a country for which astonishing strides were being accomplished (positive sentiment), and in the second, it was a country in which extreme lengths were taken to deal with what Trump believes is a crisis. This is why, to explore this yet further, we can reengineer the equation to place more emphasis on verbs and adjectives than nouns. But that will be a venture for another time.

Now, why did Trump do it this way? It's a pattern like this: extremely strong positive reaction, then an equally strong negative reaction. And the contrast between them makes them *more* powerful, not less so. Think of it this way: after a sentiment score of +9, the fall to -10 is a fall of -19: 9, 8, 7, 6, 5, 4, 3, 2, 1, 0, -1, -2, -3, -4, -5, -6, -7, -8, -9, -10.

In other words: Trump (well, Trump's speechwriters) brought the audience down from a higher point (+9), not from 0, which makes the emotional fall seem more extreme. The impact? The crisis seems more critical; it seems more urgent, and more extreme. Exactly what Trump wanted to do. Not to mention the attention-grabbing nature of alternating sentiments.

Why are they so attention-grabbing? Because the "up and down" keeps the audience emotionally engaged. Finally, and we'll get into this later, loss (negative sentiment) is felt more vividly and potently than gain (positive sentiment). So not only did the speechwriters increase the size of the fall, but falls in general are felt more than gains (according to some estimates, twice as much). And now, let's move on to our third and final equation.

You can purchase *Interpersonal Communication: How to Win Clients and Influence Teams* **from this link:** <u>bit.ly/interpersonal-comm-book</u>

Bonus Chapter #4: 219-Point Speech-Writing / Presentation-Planning Checklist That Guarantees You Don't Miss Anything Absolutely Critical

Do I engineer elements into the speech that serve to connect me to my audience?	Yes / No / Don't need
Do I engineer elements into the speech that serve to connect my audience to my idea?	Yes / No / Don't need
Do I engineer elements into the speech that serve to connect my idea to myself?	Yes / No / Don't need
Do I clearly point out the importance of the subject of my speech to my audience, if it isn't obvious?	Yes / No / Don't need
Do I have a clear speech structure that supports my message?	Yes / No / Don't need
Do I have too much information written down to possibly convey it all in my time limit?	Yes / No / Don't need
Do I only try to convey a	Yes / No / Don't need

reasonable number of ideas?	
Does my speech have an underlying theme that acts as a common thread from beginning to end?	Yes / No / Don't need
Do I have a strong opening that builds a positive first impression?	Yes / No / Don't need
Do I use transitions appropriately to provide contextual and introductory information to my audience?	Yes / No / Don't need
Do I have a hook?	Yes / No / Don't need
Is my hook early in my speech?	Yes / No / Don't need
Is my hook impactful?	Yes / No / Don't need
Does my hook echo the sentiments of my speech, and does it fit in with the rest of my speech?	Yes / No / Don't need
Does my hook point out the relevance of my subject to everyone in the audience?	Yes / No / Don't need
Does my hook establish urgency or immediacy?	Yes / No / Don't need
Do I have a call to action?	Yes / No / Don't need
Is my call to action a direct request or imperative statement?	Yes / No / Don't need
Is my call to action reasonable?	Yes / No / Don't need
If I received such a call to action after a speech like mine, would I do it?	Yes / No / Don't need

Is my call to action coming after I have successfully persuaded, informed, or inspired my audience?	Yes / No / Don't need
Do I use pathos?	Yes / No / Don't need
Do I use ethos?	Yes / No / Don't need
Do I have personal ethos?	Yes / No / Don't need
Do I use logos?	Yes / No / Don't need
Do I use pathos, ethos, and logos in a way that is mutually supportive?	Yes / No / Don't need
Do I use reciprocity?	Yes / No / Don't need
Do I use scarcity?	Yes / No / Don't need
Do I use authority?	Yes / No / Don't need
Do I use consistency?	Yes / No / Don't need
Do I use likability?	Yes / No / Don't need
Do I use consensus?	Yes / No / Don't need
If I try to establish personal authority or personal ethos, do I do so in a humble way?	Yes / No / Don't need
Is Kairos on my side?	Yes / No / Don't need
If Kairos is not on my side, is it possible for me to wait for it to be on my side?	Yes / No / Don't need
Do I tap into the core human drive of getting?	Yes / No / Don't need
Do I tap into the core human drive of bonding?	Yes / No / Don't need

Do I tap into the core human drive of learning?	Yes / No / Don't need
Do I tap into the core human drive of defending?	Yes / No / Don't need
Do I tap into the core human drive of feeling?	Yes / No / Don't need

Do I tap into the core human drive of self-actualization?	Yes / No / Don't need
Do I use statistics to support my claims?	Yes / No / Don't need
Do I use appropriate logos and logical warrants to clearly connect statistics to my main claim?	Yes / No / Don't need
Am I avoiding a non sequitur when using a statistic?	Yes / No / Don't need
Am I avoiding the impression of a non sequitur when using a statistic?	Yes / No / Don't need
Does the relevance of my statistic to my main claim stand on its own, or do I need to deliberately point it out?	Yes / No / Don't need
Do I explain the significance of a statistic after I present it?	Yes / No / Don't need
Do I use Monroe's Motivated Sequence?	Yes / No / Don't need
If not, do I still have elements designed to grab attention?	Yes / No / Don't need
If not, do I still have elements designed to present a need?	Yes / No / Don't need

If not, do I still have elements designed to present my idea, solution, or subject as a satisfaction of a need?	Yes / No / Don't need
If not, do I still have elements designed to build positive visualizations of the results of my proposal?	Yes / No / Don't need
If not, do I still have elements designed to spur my audience to action?	Yes / No / Don't need
Do I use the informational motivated sequence?	Yes / No / Don't need
If not, and if I am giving an informational speech, do I still have elements designed to persuade my audience that my information is worth listening to?	Yes / No / Don't need
Do I use the agree, promise, preview method?	Yes / No / Don't need
If not, do I still have elements designed to show understanding and empathy to my audience early in the speech?	Yes / No / Don't need
If not, do I still have elements designed to show my audience that I have a valuable solution for them early in my speech?	Yes / No / Don't need
If not, do I still have elements designed to tease part of a valuable or desirable piece of information to my audience early in my speech?	Yes / No / Don't need
If not, do I still have trust-building elements early in my speech?	Yes / No / Don't need

Do I use a concession?	Yes / No / Don't need
Is my concession brief?	Yes / No / Don't need
Do I use the proper concession format to actually launch into benefits of my alternative?	Yes / No / Don't need
If I do not use a concession, do I have another element early in my speech designed to show a level of impartiality?	Yes / No / Don't need
Do I avoid the ad hominem fallacy? (Arguing against the character of the opposition)	Yes / No / Don't need
Do I avoid the bandwagon fallacy? ("A lot of people believe it, so it's true!")	Yes / No / Don't need
Do I avoid the strawman fallacy? (Arguing against a misunderstanding of your opponent's argument)	Yes / No / Don't need
Do I avoid the appeal to authority? ("Authority figures believe it, so it's true!")	Yes / No / Don't need
Do I avoid the one or the other fallacy? (Saying that you have to choose between two things when you can do both)	Yes / No / Don't need
Do I avoid the hasty generalization fallacy? (Accepting something as true with insufficient evidence)	Yes / No / Don't need
Do I avoid the slothful induction fallacy? (Not accepting something as true with sufficient evidence)	Yes / No / Don't need

Do I avoid the correlation causation fallacy? (Before, therefore because)	Yes / No / Don't need
Do I avoid the anecdotal evidence fallacy? ("This personal story of mine proves the general rule!")	Yes / No / Don't need
Do I avoid the middle ground fallacy? ("The truth is the compromise between the two sides!)	Yes / No / Don't need
Do I avoid the burden of proof fallacy? ("I'm right unless you can prove me wrong!")	Yes / No / Don't need
Do I avoid the appeal to ignorance fallacy? ("We don't really know anything…")	Yes / No / Don't need
Do I avoid the slippery slope fallacy? ("If we do X, it will lead to Y, Y will lead to Z, Z to W, W to P, P to F, and F to I, where I is a terrible result)	Yes / No / Don't need
Do I avoid the circular argument fallacy? (Producing argumentation that internally assumes the conclusion is already proven true)	Yes / No / Don't need
Do I avoid the red herring fallacy? (Introducing irrelevant distractions)	Yes / No / Don't need
Do I avoid the sunk-cost fallacy? ("We've already spent this much money on this, might as well finish it even though it's not profitable anymore.")	Yes / No / Don't need

Do I avoid the equivocal fallacy?	Yes / No / Don't need

(Using a word in two different ways, interchanging the two meanings at will)	
Do I avoid the appeal to pity? ("Think about the victims of this! How could you do this to them?")	Yes / No / Don't need
Do I avoid the spotlight fallacy? (This recent piece of evidence is in the spotlight, therefore weighed more than evidence not getting attention)	Yes / No / Don't need
Do I avoid the appeal to tradition fallacy? ("It's how we've always been doing things, so it's the right way!")	Yes / No / Don't need
Do I use anaphora to emphasize particular phrases and build rhythm?	Yes / No / Don't need
Do I use epistrophe to place particular emphasis on a repeated word at the end of successive sentences?	Yes / No / Don't need
Do I use symploce to combine the effects of anaphora and epistrophe?	Yes / No / Don't need
Do I use antithesis, or contrasting phrases?	Yes / No / Don't need
Do I have varied and interesting sentence structure?	Yes / No / Don't need
Do I mix short, punchy phrases with longer, cascading sentences?	Yes / No / Don't need
Do I use rhetorical questions?	Yes / No / Don't need

Do I place key words and phrases at the beginning and ending of sentences?	Yes / No / Don't need
Do I use alliteration to create an explosive, punchy sentence?	Yes / No / Don't need
Do I use anadiplosis to paint sequential causes and effect relationships?	Yes / No / Don't need
Do I use asyndeton to heighten pace and intensity?	Yes / No / Don't need
Do I use polysyndeton to lengthen the size of a list of items and increase its perceived significance when it suits me?	Yes / No / Don't need
Do I use aposiopesis to rapidly gain attention and tease a big reveal to my audience?	Yes / No / Don't need
Do I use catachresis to paint unconventional, powerful, and vivid metaphors?	Yes / No / Don't need
Do I use sententia after a longer segment to give a simple mental "anchor" statement to my audience?	Yes / No / Don't need
Do I use apposition to re-root ideas in the minds of my audience?	Yes / No / Don't need

Do I replace pronouns like "they," "this," "that," "there," etc. with what the pronouns actually refer to?	Yes / No / Don't need
Do I use climax to arrange tricolon	Yes / No / Don't need

sentences or lists in order of increasing intensity?	
Do I use enumeratio to divide a word up into many parts and create a more vivid, complete, descriptive picture?	Yes / No / Don't need
Do I use epizeuxis to emphatically repeat a key phrase?	Yes / No / Don't need
Do I use diacope to emphasize a key phrase and the intervening words?	Yes / No / Don't need
Do I use parallelism to create flowing, pleasing, and beautiful rhythm?	Yes / No / Don't need
Do I use parallelism to create grammatically similar sentences with contrasting meanings?	Yes / No / Don't need
Do I use scesis onamaton to add nuance and different layers of meaning to a phrase or subject?	Yes / No / Don't need
Do I use conduplicatio to emphasize a key word or phrase that is vital to my message?	Yes / No / Don't need
Do I use expletives to interject words or phrases that relate myself or my audience back to the subject?	Yes / No / Don't need
Do I use litotes for ironic, cynical humor?	Yes / No / Don't need
Do I use attached adjectives to cement elements of my core message in the minds of my audience?	Yes / No / Don't need

Do I use antimetabole to create intuitive turns of phrase?	Yes / No / Don't need
Do I use oxymoron to highlight apparent contradictions?	Yes / No / Don't need
Do I use tricolons to create satisfying sentence structure?	Yes / No / Don't need
Do I use ascending tricolons?	Yes / No / Don't need
Do I use descending tricolons?	Yes / No / Don't need
Do I use metaphors?	Yes / No / Don't need
Do I use similes?	Yes / No / Don't need
Do I use analogies?	Yes / No / Don't need

Do I use unnecessarily complex diction?	Yes / No / Don't need
Is my diction natural?	Yes / No / Don't need
Is my diction casual for a conversational speech?	Yes / No / Don't need
Is my diction more formal for a formal speech?	Yes / No / Don't need
Do I properly omit contractions in a formal speech?	Yes / No / Don't need
Do I avoid the passive voice in favor of the active voice?	Yes / No / Don't need
Do I have a high or low substance score?	Yes / No / Don't need
Should I prioritize substance score, or style?	Yes / No / Don't need
If I want a high substance score, do	Yes / No / Don't need

I use succinct phrases?	
If I want a high substance score, do I present successive instances of contextual information?	Yes / No / Don't need
If I want a high substance score, do I use very little repetition?	Yes / No / Don't need
If I want a high substance score, do I logically present information and use lists as often as possible?	Yes / No / Don't need
If I want a high substance score, do I remove unnecessary words?	Yes / No / Don't need
Is the subject of my speech sufficiently novel to my audience?	Yes / No / Don't need
Within my speech, do I provide sufficient novelty to my audience?	Yes / No / Don't need
Do I avoid instances in my speech of going too far in depth on one exhausted subject, instead of moving on to a more novel one?	Yes / No / Don't need
Do I use refresher phrases?	Yes / No / Don't need
Do I use positive language?	Yes / No / Don't need
Do I use inclusive language?	Yes / No / Don't need
Do I see the world through my audience's eyes, and describe what I see?	Yes / No / Don't need

Do I describe relatable experiences that my audience can understand?	Yes / No / Don't need
Do I speak in terms of my audience's interests?	Yes / No / Don't need

Do I speak not only my mind, but my audience's mind?	Yes / No / Don't need
Do I use audience identifiers?	Yes / No / Don't need
Do I replace exclusive pronouns like "me and you," with inclusive pronouns like "us and we?"	Yes / No / Don't need
Do I say "we," instead of "I," to group myself with my audience when it is grammatically and factually correct to do so?	Yes / No / Don't need
Is my subject salient?	Yes / No / Don't need
Does my subject possess intensity?	Yes / No / Don't need
Does my subject possess stability?	Yes / No / Don't need
Does my subject have saliency, intensity and stability?	Yes / No / Don't need
If not, do I engineer a connection from my subject to one that is intense, stable, and salient?	Yes / No / Don't need
If my subject is not salient, intense, or stable, but rather permissive, do I use this to create saliency, stability, or intensity in my audience in whatever direction I want to?	Yes / No / Don't need
If my subject is divisive, does my speech mitigate the alienation of part of my audience?	Yes / No / Don't need
If my subject has consensus, do I acknowledge the consensus?	Yes / No / Don't need
If my subject has consensus and I am going against the consensus, is	Yes / No / Don't need

my speech adjusted accordingly?	
Do I have a clear subject?	Yes / No / Don't need
Do I have a clear theme?	Yes / No / Don't need
Does my theme become self-evident throughout my speech?	Yes / No / Don't need
Do I approach my subject with a theme that is not usually expected when dealing with my subject matter, but that is intuitive and powerful?	Yes / No / Don't need
Do I have theme to subject alignment?	Yes / No / Don't need

Is my theme positive?	Yes / No / Don't need
Do I use frame elevation?	Yes / No / Don't need
Do I use frame specification?	Yes / No / Don't need
Do I use frame presentation?	Yes / No / Don't need
Do I use frame reassertion?	Yes / No / Don't need
Do I avoid operating in a subframe?	Yes / No / Don't need
Do I use hardening techniques to create jarring segments of my speech?	Yes / No / Don't need
Do I use softening techniques to create more palatable segments when I want to?	Yes / No / Don't need
Do I avoid neutral statements when a hardened or softened statement might be better?	Yes / No / Don't need

Is my speech simple?	Yes / No / Don't need
Do I avoid any unnecessary content?	Yes / No / Don't need
Can I summarize my message in one sentence?	Yes / No / Don't need
Do I avoid the use of trade jargon?	Yes / No / Don't need
Do I use simple language?	Yes / No / Don't need
Do I compress my speech to avoid unnecessary information and words?	Yes / No / Don't need
Do I always present information in the most simple way possible?	Yes / No / Don't need
Do I use a priming statement?	Yes / No / Don't need
Do I include an element of suspense in my priming statement?	Yes / No / Don't need
Do I use personal anecdotes?	Yes / No / Don't need
If my speech is formal, do I use formal diction?	Yes / No / Don't need

If my speech is conversational, do I use conversational diction?	Yes / No / Don't need
If my speech is informational, does the structure support the clear delivery of information?	Yes / No / Don't need
If my speech is informational, do I organize the information in a pyramidal structure?	Yes / No / Don't need
If my speech is informational, do I allow for tangential pieces of	Yes / No / Don't need

information?	
If my speech is informational, is there one main thematic takeaway that is supported throughout?	Yes / No / Don't need
If my speech is informational, do I simply inform, or tell stories through which the information is easily imparted?	Yes / No / Don't need
If my speech is persuasive, do I avoid the hard-sell?	Yes / No / Don't need
If my speech is persuasive, and I am proposing a solution, do I thoroughly describe the problem I am trying to solve?	Yes / No / Don't need
If my speech is persuasive, do I include a damaging admission?	Yes / No / Don't need
If my speech is inspirational, do I use positive persuasion?	Yes / No / Don't need
If my speech is inspirational, do I use negative persuasion?	Yes / No / Don't need
If my speech is inspirational, do I use more positive persuasion than negative persuasion?	Yes / No / Don't need
If my speech is inspirational, do I appeal to loss aversion?	Yes / No / Don't need
Have I made sure that my speech fits in the allotted time, with a cushion?	Yes / No / Don't need
Do I have opening and closing pleasantries?	Yes / No / Don't need
Do I never criticize, condemn, or	Yes / No / Don't need

complain in my speech?	
Do I give honest and sincere appreciation in my speech?	Yes / No / Don't need
Do I arouse in the audience an eager want to follow my call to action?	Yes / No / Don't need
Do I make my audience happy about following my call to action?	Yes / No / Don't need
Do I give my audience honest and sincere appreciation?	Yes / No / Don't need

Do I speak in terms of the audience's interests?	Yes / No / Don't need
Am I sympathetic to the audience's ideas and desires?	Yes / No / Don't need
Do I get the audience thinking "yes," multiple times, in a "yes-ladder," immediately?	Yes / No / Don't need
Do I appeal to the nobler motives?	Yes / No / Don't need
Do I dramatize my ideas?	Yes / No / Don't need
Do I throw down a challenge?	Yes / No / Don't need
Do I talk about my own mistakes before criticizing or pointing out the mistakes of my audience?	Yes / No / Don't need
Do I call attention to my audience's mistakes indirectly?	Yes / No / Don't need
Do I use encouragement and make the audience's faults, or the problem I am discussing, seem easy to correct?	Yes / No / Don't need

Do I tap into audience emotion?	Yes / No / Don't need
Do I use emotive language, or language with emotional connotations?	Yes / No / Don't need
Do I use language that expresses conviction?	Yes / No / Don't need
Do I replace weak phrases like "might," "may," and "could," with strong absolutes like "will?"	Yes / No / Don't need
Do I assert my ideas across the past, present, and future?	Yes / No / Don't need
Am I ready to give the greatest, most impressive, most ground-breaking, earth-shattering, beautiful, incredible, powerful speech that has ever graced humanity?	Yes / No / Don't need

YOUR LINK TO YOUR FREE RESOURCES AND VIDEO COURSE:
www.publicspeakinghub.com/free-resources

Made in the USA
Columbia, SC
19 August 2021

43971685R00111